943
Hin

6530

DISCARDED

6530

6530

DATE DUE	BORROWER'S NAME	

943   **Hintz, Martin**
HIN   **West Germany**

02793-X

943   Hintz, Martin
HIN   West Germany

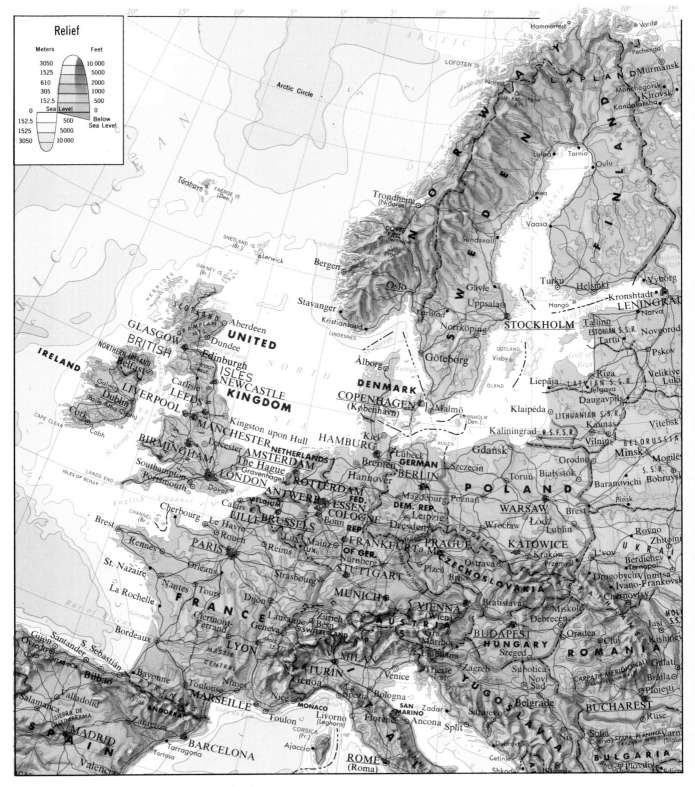

Scale 1:4 000 000; one inch to 64 miles. Conic Projection
Elevations and depressions are given in feet.

Enchantment of the World

WEST GERMANY

By Martin Hintz

Consultant: Bruce Broerman, Ph.D., Assistant Professor, Department of German, University of Illinois at Chicago

Consultant for Social Studies: Donald W. Nylin, Ph.D., Assistant Superintendent for Instruction, Aurora West Public Schools, Aurora, Illinois

Consultant for Reading: Robert L. Hillerich, Ph.D., Bowling Green State University, Bowling Green, Ohio

CHILDRENS PRESS ™

CHICAGO

*Pottenstein,
Bavaria*

**This book is dedicated to the Hintz and Baum families on my father's side. They
came to the United States seeking a new vision and a new freedom—but still
retained their love of homeland, culture, and tradition. They epitomized the best of
what Germany was and is.**

Special thanks for their help in the preparation of this book are extended to Hedy
Wuerz and Hans J. Baumann, German National Tourist Board; tourism personnel
across Germany, especially West Berliner Bernhard Troll and Hubertus W. Hillig of
Hamburg; the Press and Information Office of the Federal Republic of Germany; the
Federal Ministry of Food, Agriculture, and Forestry; the German Information Center;
Hans J. Rathje, Inter-View Communications, Inc.; my sister Gretchen Wronka and her
husband, Guenther; Hans Nykanp of AD-PRO Concepts; and Karl Koepcke of
Lufthansa German Airlines. Extra thanks are offered to the dozens of wonderful
German friends I have met, from Lübeck to Berchtesgaden, who have opened their
homes and their hearts in sharing the delights of their country.

Picture Acknowledgments
German National Tourist Office, Chicago: Cover
Colour Library International: Pages 4, 8, 9, 10, 16, 17, 19,
22, 46, 54 (top left), 56, 62 (top), 64 (top left and bottom
right), 65 (center left), 81, 86, 101, 104, 105 (right)
Chandler Forman: Pages 5, 41, 55 (left), 73
German Information Center, New York: Pages 6, 12, 13,
15, 49, 50, 51, 52, 54 (bottom), 57, 58, 61, 64 (bottom left),
65 (bottom and center right), 66, 68, 69, 70, 71, 76, 78
(bottom), 89, 90, 92, 93 (top left, bottom left, and bottom
right), 100, 102, 103, 105 (left), 106, 109
Historical Pictures Service, Inc., Chicago: Pages 28, 32, 78
U.S. Army Photograph SC 661743: Page 38
Hillstrom Stock Photos/© Robert Mohn: Pages 40, 55
(right), 91
Martin Hintz: Pages 53, 95 (top right)
© David J. Maenza: Page 54 (top right)
Irene E. Hubbell: Page 62 (bottom), 65 (top)
National Tourist Office, Cologne: Page 64 (top right)
Len Meents: Maps on pages 25, 31, and 34, based on Rand
McNally maps; maps on pages 50, 56, 57, 61, 62
**Courtesy Flag Research Center, Winchester,
Massachusetts 01890:** Flag on back cover
Cover: Rheinstein, one of the most beautiful castles on the
Rhine River

Library of Congress Cataloging in Publication Data

Hintz, Martin.
   West Germany.

   (Enchantment of the world)
   Includes index.
   Summary: Discusses the geography, history, culture,
and economy of Germany.
   1. Germany (West)—Juvenile literature.
[1. Germany (West)] I. Title. II. Series.
DD259.H48   1983   943   82-17882
ISBN-0-516-02793-X   AACR2

Frau Maria Baer sells radishes near the cathedral in Regensburg.

TABLE OF CONTENTS

A Bavarian brass band marches down a Munich street.

Chapter 1

GUTEN TAG,
DEUTSCHLAND

Test time!

Is it true that the Federal Republic of Germany is only a land of oompah bands, beer, and hand-carved clocks? Do all German men wear *Lederhosen,* those leather shorts that look best when stained with *Spanferkel* grease? Do all German women have blond braids and bake fantastic, mile-high strawberry tortes? German history is full of flags and marching soldiers—good material for late-night war movies. Right?

If you answered "yes" to all these questions, you would be mostly wrong. Germany is such a mixture of so many diverse elements that it is impossible to say that "all Germans do this" or that "all the country's history" is the stuff of films.

Remember that there are actually two Germanys. The Federal Republic is more commonly called West Germany. The German Democratic Republic is known as East Germany. These two independent nations were born after World War II, when the West retained about 53 percent of the land and the East 23 percent.

The golden fountain on the grounds of Schloss Linderhof in Bavaria sends a towering spray of water into the air.

Another chunk of prewar Germany was absorbed by Poland and the Soviet Union.

West Germany is made up of the areas that were controlled by Britain, France, and the United States at the end of World War II. The Eastern territories were taken over by the Soviet Union. The two Germanys still differ sharply in politics today.

Though there are two Germanys, in this book most of our story will focus on today's West Germany.

This nation is swept up in three time levels: the past, the present, and the future. West Germany is a land of castles and industry, of fairy tales and science, of history and plans for tomorrow.

The country has always been a trading center and industrial hub because of its location in Europe. It is certain to retain that important position, for it remains a major crossing point between East and West.

The onion-domed Church of Maria Gern in Bavaria

The Germans are lucky to have an abundance of art, architecture, music, and crafts that are typically their own. Baroque art masterpieces, sweeping operas, and towering church spires delight the senses in many places. The land is just as rich in natural delights: parks, waterways, mountains, woodlands, the sea. Germany is a delightful blend of human energy and nature: outdoor concerts, plays set in the hills, and sporting events under the blue dome of the sky.

After the war, much of West Germany lay in ruins. But with help from Western powers, its people made a fresh start, blending the best of its past into today's fast-paced world. Today's young Germans are products of that sort of society.

Mittenwald, Bavaria

Chapter 2

A GEOGRAPHY
OF EXCITEMENT

West Germany lies in the heartland of the European continent. The country's only natural frontiers are the sea along parts of the northern boundary and the mountains in the south. Denmark borders Germany on the north as well, with The Netherlands (Holland), Belgium, Luxembourg, and France on the west. To the south are Austria and Switzerland. Czechoslovakia is to the southeast. Directly east is the German Democratic Republic (East Germany), which in turn is bordered farther east by Poland.

The country's outline somewhat resembles a misshapen half moon. It curves westward from its northern and southern frontiers. In the center East Germany pushes inward from the east. West Germany is 562 miles long (900 kilometers) from north to south. It is about 250 miles (400 kilometers) from east to west at its widest point.

There are at least five very distinctive types of landscape within West Germany. Each district has its own traditions, life-styles, and dialects—which have been shaped by the surrounding terrain. A

Hamburg is one of the major cities in the northern plains.

visitor traveling through West Germany would see the northern plains, the central mountain ranges, the hills of the west and south, the south German Alpine foothills, and the Bavarian Alps. Nearly one third of this entire area is covered with forests.

THE NORTHERN PLAINS

Let's look first at the northern plains. This vast, rolling stretch of countryside runs across Germany from east to west. It was probably formed by the movement of glaciers many thousands of years ago. Those frosty landscapers created a fertile farming area by piling up rich soil, extending from the Jutland peninsula past the Lüneburg Heath, south of the major city of Hamburg. Where great ice packs once growled, sheep now roam in large flocks over grassy meadows.

Flensburg is one of the main towns on West Germany's border with Denmark. Denmark can be seen in the background of this picture.

Some of the ice was buried by sand as the glaciers retreated. As the leftover underground ice melted, potholes were formed. They eventually became large and small lakes, many of which are great for recreational swimming, boating, and fishing. Stone Age people who lived in those ancient times might have splashed happily in the same pools. Numerous resorts and spas have been built where those early people foraged for food. Today's Germans enjoy the healthful mud and brine baths that can be found all over the area.

The major cities in the northern plains are Hamburg, Kiel, Bremen, and Lübeck. Flensburg is one of the main towns on the border with Denmark. From these trading centers businesspeople have ventured forth through the ages to conquer the world's money markets.

THE CENTRAL MOUNTAINS

The southern edge of the plains blends into a succession of ancient mountains that form the backbone of West Germany. The mountains have picturesque names—the Harz, the Teutoburger Wald, the Rhön, the Taunus, the Rheinisches Schiefergebirge (Rhineland slate mountains), and the Rothaargebirge.

These aren't typical craggy mountains, because they are so old and worn from erosion. Actually, the Germans call them the Uplands. They've been wave-battered by the ocean that once flooded this whole region millions of years ago, and they've been buffeted by younger volcanoes. When people first started roaming through these rugged hills, they found deposits of lead, zinc, copper, and silver. The Harz Mountains were especially rich in these minerals. A great deal of coal is still mined along the eastern edge of the Uplands.

Much of this rocky rib cage of Germany is forested, heavily covered with spruce, oak, and beech trees.

Cities in this region include Goslar, Kassel, and Vogelsberg. There are also many tiny hamlets and villages tucked into the cracks and crevasses of the old mountain ranges and in the broad valleys that separate the ridges.

THE SOUTHERN HILL COUNTRY
AND THE BLACK FOREST

The southern hill country is just high enough to let hikers begin to stretch their leg muscles. This is a lovely tourist region. There are many excellent hotels and restaurants in the Black Forest, which blankets the land. The Black Forest received its name

Goslar (above) is a city in the Harz Mountains. The Externsteine (below) are natural rock formations in the Teutoburger Wald that were used by the ancient Celts as a moon observatory.

The Black Forest blankets the southern hill country of West Germany.

because the trees are so numerous and so close that little light can filter through the leaves.

The severe climate of the Ice Age shattered and broke huge chunks of rock that still can be seen littering the valleys. In the Odenwald, some of the accessible sandstone was quarried by the Romans and used for towering pillars for their temples and other structures in Italy.

This rugged southern German landscape provides a key route for such major rivers as the Rhine, which meanders along between the cliffs. Some of the finest farmland in West Germany is in the valleys here.

*The Zugspitze,
near Garmisch-
Partenkirchen,
is one of the
highest Alpine peaks.*

THE BAVARIAN ALPS

The southern hills merge into the Alpine foothills, many of which are plateaus. The foothills were ground down by glaciers. The numerous pockets that remained filled with melting snow and eventually became lakes. One of the most interesting of these is Lake Constance, also called Bodensee. It's an enormous lake straddling West Germany's borders with Austria and Switzerland. Mainau, a large island just offshore, has a climate warm enough to allow tropical plants to grow. This is a prime resort area.

Next come the Alps, those soaring mountains that seem made for picture postcards. However, only a small portion of the Alps actually lies within West Germany. Most of the mountains stretch through Austria, Switzerland, and on into France.

Yet Germany has one of the highest Alpine peaks, the Zugspitze, which soars 9,721 feet (2,963 meters) into the sky.

Hearty climbers can scramble up a rocky path to the crest, where they can see over the mountains into Austria. Of course, it's easier to take a cogwheel train (a tiny mountain trolley) and then board a cable car partway up for the rest of the ride to the top.

Munich is the major city in the foothills of the Bavarian Alps. The tallest mountains are only a short drive from the center of town. Another famous village here is Oberammergau, site of the world-famous Passion Play that depicts the last days of Christ. The resorts of Mittenwald and Garmisch-Partenkirchen are well known; so is Berchtesgaden, home of many famous wood-carvers and fancy spas.

With Bavaria's colorful combination of sky, snow, and mist, it's no wonder the people of the district love their blue and white flag.

THE FOUR SEASONS

The climatic changes in West Germany go hand in hand with the landscape. Of course, it's usually cooler and fresher on a summer day in the Alps than in a valley of central Germany. Some of the best weather of the year occurs in spring, especially from March through May. Fields of poppies in the hills are such a bright red they glow like living fire. The clear skies are so brilliant they almost hurt your eyes.

Generally, there is a lot of ground haze and cold weather from mid-December through early February. But that doesn't stop the Germans. These are great times for Alpine skiing, sledding, and ice skating. Often, however, there is a Christmas thaw in the lowlands that turns snow to slush.

In the mountains, the snow stays crisp and new throughout the entire winter, often piling higher than the tops of cars. Lodges,

Thick beams support the roof of this farmhouse near Reit-im-Winkl in Upper Bavaria.

houses, and barns have to have very thick beams to support their roofs. Otherwise a family might have a living room full of snow because the ceiling collapsed under all that weight!

April is the messiest month. It rains and rains and rains. There is nothing quite like an early spring storm that rages in across the northern German plain. It seems as if the wind could rip off your coat. Sometimes the rain turns to sleet in the Uplands, causing many traffic accidents on the slippery *Autobahnen*, the busy West German highways. But when the April sun does shine, the landscape explodes with colors. The air is crisp. Everything is freshly washed by the rain, so that the world seems to sparkle. It's a time when the windows are opened and goose-down bedding is taken out to be aired.

Summer months are unpredictable. Sometimes there is a lot of rain in June, the end of July, and the beginning of August. Vacationing schoolchildren moan and groan. Along the Rhine

River in the summer, the days are long and lazy, perfect for outings along this major waterway. It gets quite warm in southern Germany during this season, but a sudden storm thundering down from the Alps can bring cool days as well.

Autumn is one of the best seasons in Germany. Everywhere the leaves turn scarlet, orange, and yellow. The days are usually mild and comfortable. Temperatures are never really bitter cold in Germany, except in the mountains. The winter average is around 32 degrees Fahrenheit (0 degrees Celsius). Summer averages around 70 degrees Fahrenheit (21.1 degrees Celsius), which is just about right for all sorts of outdoor activities. There is snow year round on the Zugspitze.

In the mountains, skiers have to be aware of the *Föhn*. This is a very dangerous warm wind that melts the snow base on south-facing cliffs. Avalanches can result quickly because of the snow's mushy, wet heaviness.

A CHANGING ENVIRONMENT

West Germans are generally conscious of their environment and are concerned about pollution. Of course, under the pressures of the industrial age, the country is having some difficulty in keeping certain areas clean. It is estimated that the 24 million cars and trucks in West Germany annually pump into the air about 50,000 tons (45,359 metric tons) of sulfur dioxide, 350,000 tons (317,515 metric tons) of nitrogen oxide, 6.5 million tons (5.9 million metric tons) of carbon monoxide, and 250,000 tons (226,796 metric tons) of hydrocarbons.

The West German government passed the Federal Emission Protection Act in 1974, designed to help clean the air. The law covers not only cars but also factories and private dwellings. Whether it will control the pollution is still questionable.

Other regulations also have been put into effect in an attempt to lessen water pollution. It is dangerous to drink from a stream almost anywhere in West Germany. The Rhine River is very polluted. Although ten million West Germans and their Dutch neighbors use the river for drinking water, it is twenty times more polluted than it was in 1949. The government estimates that only about half of the sewage and industrial waste dumped into the river has been adequately cleaned.

There has been some success, however, especially in Bavaria, where many lakes are now clear again since better sewage treatment plants were constructed. The Bodensee was once extremely filthy but is now slowly returning to life.

Landscapes are changing as well in West Germany, as more and more open space is devoured by city suburbs and industrial growth. Many West Germans prefer to live outside of towns. This can be fine if the growth of housing is planned. But the movement to rural areas has unfortunately led to uncontrolled destruction of the countryside in several places. Ecologists are afraid that the natural state of some regions, such as areas in the Alps, has been permanently damaged. Housing and road construction, mainly to help the tourism industry, have been blamed for some of the trouble.

Yet the West Germans are doing a great deal to preserve what they have. There are fifty-five nature parks and some thirteen hundred nature reserves in the Federal Republic. A law called the *Bundesnaturschutzgesetz* (the Nature Conservation and Landscape Cultivation Act) was passed in 1976. It makes sure these properties remain protected.

Berchtesgaden (above) is only a few miles north of Mount Watzmann and Königssee, where a national park was opened in 1978.

The first German national park was opened in 1970 in the Bavarian Forest, with a second in 1978 in the Berchtesgaden Alps around Mount Watzmann and Königssee, a vast lake nearby. Several other sites also are being considered for this special status, including the north Frisian tidal flats, the Lüneburg Heath, and the Rhön area of Hesse.

It is still an uphill fight. In fact, one government statistic claims that the Federal Republic produces so much garbage every year that it could be piled as high as the Zugspitze! Everyone agrees that this is one difficulty with a society that is expanding so fast economically. The West Germans remain optimistic, however. They are sure these problems can be solved if everyone helps work toward a solution.

Chapter 3

FROM THE BEGINNING

The Germans are old. West Germany is young.

That's one way to sum up the history of these fascinating people and their country. The German heritage stretches back more than a thousand years. The modern nation of West Germany, however, is less than fifty years old. Throughout the years, the borders of what we call modern Germany have expanded and shrunk, as governments shifted and changed like the tide. Much of what was once ethnic German territory has been carved away.

The original "Germans" belonged to many wandering tribes of hunters, warriors, and herders. For generations, they battled outsiders while they expanded their own territories. Even the Romans were unable to conquer the rugged peoples who lived in the lands bordered by the Rhine, Elbe, and Danube rivers. The Germanic tribes included the Alemans, Saxons, Franks, Angles, Jutes, Frisians, Swabians, Vandals, Langobards, Burgundians, Thuringians, Ostrogoths, and Visigoths. A "German's" first loyalty was to his tribe.

When these family bands weren't farming, tending their cattle, or defending themselves from attacks, they were fighting among themselves. The Franks finally won most of the battles and thereby gained control of most of the land.

A STRONG LEADER

The Franks were led by a king named Charlemagne, which means "Charles the Great." Charlemagne's kingdom extended over the territory that comprises modern-day France and West Germany, as well as parts of Spain and Italy. He united the tribes by gentle persuasion, by massacres, and by moving whole groups from one end of his kingdom to another. He was named emperor by Pope Leo III on Christmas Day in the year A.D. 800. Charlemagne devised a series of laws under which his commanders governed their provinces, stimulated foreign trade, and settled arguments about religion.

Charlemagne thought his family would keep the kingdom unified after his death. But his offspring were not as strong as he had been, and soon various ethnic groups began fighting among themselves again. The next several emperors spent more time arguing than ruling. Eventually, various regions began breaking away from the old empire.

The Treaty of Verdun (843) divided Charlemagne's empire into three kingdoms, which went to his three grandsons. The western part of the empire was governed by Charles the Bald. Another grandson, Louis the German, took the eastern part. Between them, a corridor from the North Sea to central Italy went to a third grandson, Lothar. They divided the kingdom among themselves along what today might be called French and German lines.

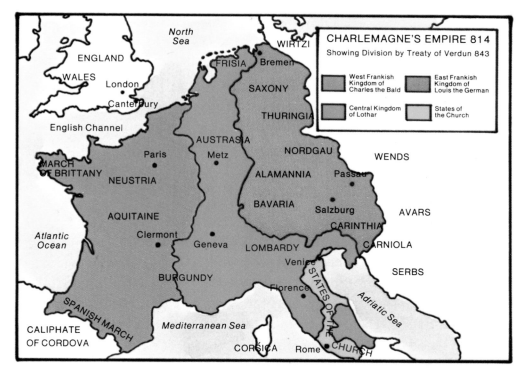

Over the next few generations, the French kings consolidated their portion of the empire. The Germans, however, kept dreaming of the old days when Charlemagne ruled the entire area. They wanted to bring back the days of the empire.

A NEW EMPIRE

In 919 Henry I of Saxony became king of the Germans. Henry's son grew up to be Otto the Great. Otto beat back the Hungarians from the south, extended Germany's borders in the north, took over the old Middle Frankish Kingdom, and had himself crowned emperor in Rome in 962. The event marked the beginning of what was later called the Holy Roman Empire.

Whether the empire was holy or not is for others to decide. But under the Saxon dynasty—the rulers descended from Otto the Great—the empire became the most powerful regime in Europe.

This state of affairs lasted until 1024. When a new dynasty, or ruling family, took over, the nobles began to fight among themselves, as nobles tended to do. During the next hundred years or so, the empire grew weak and disorganized.

CENTURIES OF FIGHTING

During those rough-and-tumble years, a number of German-speaking settlers crossed the Alps into what is now Switzerland. Others moved east, into the Slavic regions. An order of medieval Christian knights was very active in colonizing the vast stretches of plains that extend into modern-day Poland and Russia. They originally went into this territory to Christianize the Prussians. They were well-disciplined soldiers and administrators whose methods were adopted by succeeding generations of German rulers.

The entire Holy Roman Empire disintegrated into a maze of petty little nation-states that kept nipping at each other. The stronger kingdoms were located in the Danube River area, under the control of the House of Hapsburg. Some of the kings spoke French, some Italian, some German, some Latin, and some even spoke Czech.

Through marriage and military conquests, the Hapsburgs became the major rulers throughout the entire region, with some relatives controlling Burgundy, Flanders (both parts of today's France and Belgium), and Spain. The French kings didn't look kindly on all this power in the hands of a single family. The groundwork was being laid for subsequent centuries of rivalry and war between France and what would become Germany.

The peasants who lived in the villages dotting the countryside didn't care about all those political games. Beginning in the 1100s, they were forced by the nobles into a kind of slavery called serfdom. There really wasn't a German nation yet, and the people were united only by their common language.

THE RISE OF THE CITIES

As the emperors lost power, certain German cities became so big and so rich that they gained self-government. In the late 1200s they started banding together to protect themselves. Lübeck, Hamburg, Bremen, and other port cities formed an association called the Hanseatic League. The league eventually controlled most of the sea traffic around Scandinavia and set up trading centers all over the area around the North and Baltic seas. The merchants grew so wealthy, in fact, that they lent money to most of the petty kings and princes, who needed cash to finance their wars and their lavish life-styles. This was the era when many beautiful cathedrals and castles were built. Art and music flourished.

RELIGION AND POLITICS

But all was not peaceful. The serfs in the countryside had grown weary of living like slaves. People questioned abuses in the Roman Catholic church, to which everyone belonged. A number of so-called radicals and heretics took to the roads, preaching beliefs other than those taught by the established priests and bishops.

In 1517, a German monk named Martin Luther was upset by what he felt were problems in the spiritual realm. He nailed a list of ninety-five theses to the cathedral door in Wittenberg,

In 1517, German monk Martin Luther nailed a list of suggestions for church reforms on the cathedral door in Wittenberg.

asking for reforms in church practices. Although religious upheaval was already raging throughout Europe, Luther's act has often been called the official start of what is known as the Reformation.

Bloodshed in the name of religion soon followed. There were many fights among families, local princes, and even cities as the Protestant reformers sought to consolidate their power. The peasants revolted in 1524 and were brutally put down. The fighting and religious debates went on for several generations. By 1618, the conflict had become a land grab. For the next three decades, the battles continued in what is called the Thirty Years' War. Protestant German princes joined with England, Sweden, Denmark, and France against what was left of the Holy Roman Empire and the Hapsburgs, most of whom were Roman Catholic.

Much of the fighting was on German soil, exhausting the people. The Treaty of Westphalia in 1648 finally ended the horrors. But it took centuries before the suffering of those years could be put aside. The treaty limited the power of the German royalty. France and Sweden won important German territory. Brandenburg-Prussia, taking advantage of this situation, made many treaties with other nations and became the strongest German state after the war.

THE AGE OF ABSOLUTISM

Germany became a patchwork of hundreds of states ruled by princes and nobles. The new era became known as the Age of Absolutism, because the ruler of each territory was given absolute, limitless power. Each state could control all economic, political, social, and military operations within its borders. Saxony and Hanover grew to be very powerful.

Neighboring Austria, which had acquired huge chunks of Hungary and the Balkan territories, was a major rival during those days. From 1740 to 1786, the state of Prussia was consolidated under Frederick the Great.

FRANCE FLEXES ITS MUSCLES

Throughout the eighteenth century, Germany was actually a loose collection of more than 1,700 principalities (regions ruled by princes) of various sizes. In 1789, the French Revolution broke out, and armies once again tramped across Europe. Prussia and Austria attempted to turn back the tide as the French under Napoleon threatened to conquer all Europe. Napoleon took over almost 350 German principalities on the left bank of the Rhine River.

The Holy Roman Empire came to an end in 1806, when Emperor Franz II gave up Charlemagne's crown in Vienna to become the ruler of Austria-Hungary. From that time on, his German-speaking subjects thought of themselves as Austrians.

After the wars with Napoleon, a strong conservative element gained power in most of the states that remained intact in Germany. Many princes realized that eventually they would have to band together as a nation in order to keep the German people from being absorbed into other countries, as had happened in Austria.

A NEW MAP OF EUROPE

The Congress of Vienna in 1815 redrew the map of Europe. But the hopes of many Germans for a free nation were not realized. A *Deutscher Bund*, a German confederation, replaced the old mishmash of principalities. A central parliament was appointed, with representatives from the various major states. But the parliament could act only if Prussia and Austria approved of its rulings.

The capitals of the various states became very important. Prussia's Berlin was an intellectual center. Bavaria's Munich was a center for the arts. In addition, as the years went on, the various German states banded together economically. A railroad was started to link the cities. Industrialization began, with a new class of factory workers. Most of them lived in poverty, however.

Revolution again swept Europe in 1848. The German lower classes seized the chance to rebel. At first they forced many of the princes to give them new freedoms. The national assembly met to discuss how to control the situation, and agreed to seek a constitutional monarchy and allow some limited voting rights for the people. The idea of a "greater Germany" was catching on.

In 1849, a constitution was drawn up, and King Frederick William IV of Prussia was offered the imperial crown. He turned

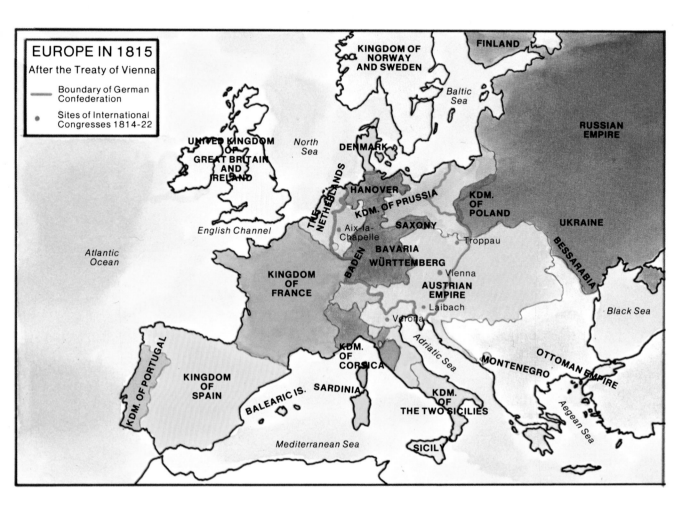

EUROPE IN 1815
After the Treaty of Vienna

— Boundary of German Confederation

• Sites of International Congresses 1814-22

FINLAND

KINGDOM OF NORWAY AND SWEDEN

Baltic Sea

RUSSIAN EMPIRE

UNITED KINGDOM OF GREAT BRITAIN AND IRELAND

North Sea

DENMARK

HANOVER

KDM. OF PRUSSIA

KDM. OF POLAND

UKRAINE

THE NETHERLANDS

Aix-la-Chapelle

SAXONY

Troppau

BESSARABIA

English Channel

BADEN

BAVARIA

WÜRTTEMBERG

Vienna

Atlantic Ocean

KINGDOM OF FRANCE

AUSTRIAN EMPIRE

Laibach

Black Sea

Verona

Adriatic Sea

KDM. OF CORSICA

MONTENEGRO

OTTOMAN EMPIRE

KDM. OF PORTUGAL

KINGDOM OF SPAIN

BALEARIC IS.

SARDINIA

KDM. OF THE TWO SICILIES

Aegean Sea

Mediterranean Sea

SICILY

it down, because he didn't want to be associated with anything
that was the result of a revolution. Immediately, the people rose
again in an attempt to enforce the new constitution. But the
German princes called out their armies. Led by the Prussians, they
crushed the rebellion and tossed out the constitution. In 1850, the
German Confederation was refounded.

*Otto von Bismarck,
the "Iron Chancellor,"
united Germany and
formed a German empire.*

BLOOD AND IRON

Prussia continued its growth under Prime Minister Otto von
Bismarck. He realized that the Confederation was weak. In 1864,
Prussia went to war with Denmark and captured the territories of
Schleswig and Holstein, which today form West Germany's most
northern state. In 1866, Bismarck defeated Austria and drew up a
treaty that dissolved the Confederation. It was replaced by the
North German Federation, the states north of the Main River.
Bismarck remained as federal chancellor.

Bismarck believed in his motto: "Blood and Iron." He fought
with France and won the territories of Alsace-Lorraine in 1871.
The southern German principalities saw how powerful the
Prussian state had become. They wanted to join Bismarck's
federation. After the defeat of France, the German princes met at
Versailles, which is near Paris. They declared that their federation
was now a *Reich*, a German empire. King Wilhelm I of Prussia
was proclaimed German emperor.

And so a German nation was finally born.

Chapter 4

FROM EMPIRE
TO DEMOCRACY

The new German empire lasted from 1871 to 1918. As long as Bismarck kept control as chancellor, the complicated system of government stayed intact. Many Germans, however, did not like the fact that Prussia had the most power in the Reich. Besides, German unity had not come about because all the people were involved equally. It basically resulted from the demands and desires of the nobility.

In the empire, all male citizens could vote for representatives to the *Reichstag,* the imperial assembly. However, the legislators did not have a real voice in the formation of the government. The formal decision-making body was the *Bundesrat,* the federal council that was the assembly of representatives appointed by the princes. The chancellor—Bismarck—did not have to report to either group. He was responsible only to the emperor, called the *Kaiser.*

Still, Germany prospered under Prussian direction. It became heavily industrialized and signed peace treaties with other

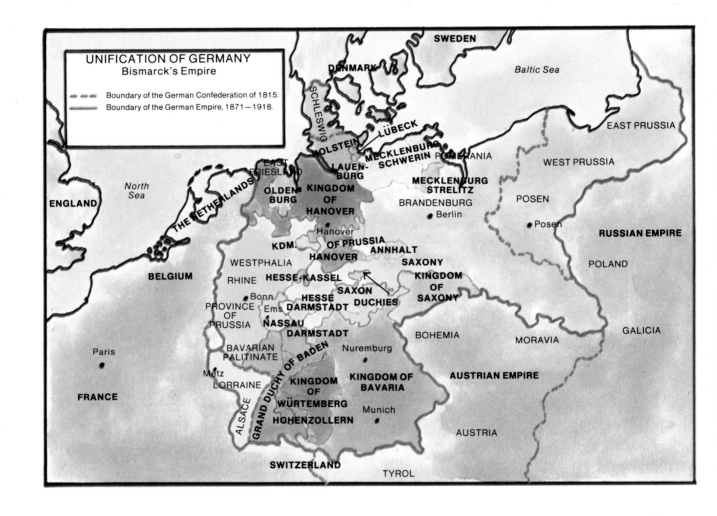

countries. Through these pacts, Germany began acquiring colonies
in Africa and in the Pacific, joining other European nations in a
mad rush for new territories. The country developed a huge navy
to keep watch over its overseas possessions.

Despite Germany's growing wealth and its rising position in

world affairs, the average citizen did not feel represented by the government. Even some enlightened social legislation did not help. Bismarck simply thought that anyone who opposed him was wrong. The nobility, especially those in the military, agreed. The middle class, the Catholics, and the labor unions were often at odds with the rulers of Germany. In 1878, two attempts were made on Kaiser Wilhelm's life. These led to many measures aimed at putting down opposition to the government. Underneath the smooth surface of German life, trouble was brewing.

THE END OF AN ERA

Kaiser Wilhelm died in 1888 and was succeeded by his son, Frederick II. Frederick, however, ruled for only four months; he died of cancer of the throat soon after taking power and was succeeded by his son, Wilhelm II.

Bismarck and the new kaiser did not like each other. Chancellor Bismarck was fired and spent the rest of his life writing criticisms of Wilhelm II.

The affairs of Germany were not managed well after Bismarck left office. Wilhelm II wanted to govern by himself, but he wasn't very good at it. He made many speeches championing Germany as a leading voice in world affairs. This, of course, frightened other European nations. They had already noticed Germany's rapid expansion. The country's population grew from forty-one to sixty-one million in forty years and German industrial might was being felt around the world. Then there was the threat of Germany's quest for more colonies. Soon, Germany found itself almost isolated, except for treaties with Austria and Italy that had somehow remained intact since Bismarck's time.

A WORLD AT WAR

On June 28, 1914, Archduke Francis Ferdinand of Austria-Hungary and his wife were murdered. The assassination of the archduke triggered the start of World War I. Though Germany had very little to do with the conditions leading to the conflict, certain German leaders saw the war as a chance to gain more territory. But so did Germany's neighbors.

The war ground on and on, costing millions of lives. Wilhelm retreated into the background. His officers took over in a virtual military dictatorship under Field Marshal Paul von Hindenburg and General Erich Ludendorff.

Germany eventually was crushed by the combined might of the major nations of the world, including the United States, Russia, France, Great Britain, and Italy. The German economy was in ruins, the people were dispirited, and the rulers were in disgrace. The kaiser and all the princes stepped down from power. Another system of government had to be found.

In the peace drawn up at Versailles, the winning nations demanded that Germany become a republic. Germany also had to pay for the cost of the war. There was mass unemployment, inflation that made German money worthless, and protests from starving and angry veterans. Large portions of prewar Germany were handed over to France, Poland, and other countries. Germany had to give up its colonies. It was a very sad time for the Germans.

The Social Democrats became the strongest political party in postwar Germany. Some of the politicians sought to make an orderly change from the old to the new form of state, but it was very hard. The important businesspeople and the landowners kept control of the factories and the farms. The officer corps in the military remained elite. Attempts to distribute power and wealth more equally were put down by the army. Everyone was arguing; no one was working together. The 1920s were terrible years for the Germans.

On top of all these problems, Germany was hit by the Great Depression, an economic catastrophe that affected the entire world. By the early 1930s, many businesses had failed and six million Germans were out of work. Life in Germany was even worse than it had been immediately after the First World War.

It didn't take long before the republic collapsed. There was too much pressure from all sides. The scene was set for a dictator.

THE RISE OF HITLER

From 1930 on, the National Socialist movement of Adolf Hitler slowly gained control over all political processes in Germany. Hitler and his followers were able to take advantage of the country's turmoil. They used violence and terror to get what they wanted.

Hitler was an Austrian who had fought in the Bavarian army during World War I. After the war, he joined the German Workers' party, which eventually became the National Socialists, or Nazis. Hitler blamed the country's woes on Jews, Communists, and everyone else who disagreed with him. In 1923, he and several hundred followers attempted to take over the government in what was called the "Beer Hall Putsch." This attempt failed, and Hitler went to prison for nine months. There he wrote his famous book *Mein Kampf* ("My Struggle"). The essays related how he felt about the world around him. It was a very grim story.

Adolf Hitler, a very effective public speaker, waved to this cheering crowd from the balcony of the Reich Chancery as a beaming Field Marshal Hermann Goering looked on.

Hitler was a very effective public speaker, and he was able to get large crowds to support him. In 1933, he was appointed chancellor of Germany. He soon got rid of the conservative allies who had helped put him in office. He was given practically unlimited power and he used it ruthlessly. He jailed political opponents, banned trade unions, and abolished freedom of the press. He called himself *der Führer* ("the Leader") and claimed his Reich would last a thousand years. Hitler had become a dictator.

After Hitler seized power, there was little to stop him from doing away with the Jewish people, the gypsies, and anyone else he felt was not a "pure" German ethnically. In 1934, he became president of the German republic and commander of the armed forces, in addition to being chancellor.

Although many Germans resisted this takeover, there were not enough to stop Hitler. The idea of democracy had not taken very firm root in the terrible days after World War I. Besides, the common people had not had much voice in their government before the war. When Hitler came to power, people noticed only that jobs were plentiful again. Who cared if that was because ammunition factories were in full swing?

Even Germans who should have realized what was happening were impressed with Hitler's grasp of international politics. He was able to take over Austria and Czechoslovakia and gain back some territory lost after World War I. This gave many Germans a feeling that their country had become powerful again. Hitler called the Germans a superior race of people, which gave him an excuse for persecuting opponents of the Reich.

THE SECOND WORLD WAR

Bolstered by these successes, Hitler's troops invaded Poland on September 1, 1939, launching World War II. The war lasted almost six years and cost at least fifty-five million lives. After Poland, German armies quickly invaded and conquered Denmark, Norway, Holland, Belgium, France, Yugoslavia, and Greece. They advanced nearly to Moscow in the Soviet Union and controlled most of North Africa. Hitler was aided by allies such as Italy, and was helped by the warring Japanese on the other side of the globe. It seemed as if he could not lose.

Concentration camps, where many millions of innocent people were put to death, sprang up all over the occupied territories. In

*On the gate of the Dachau concentration camp was the ironic slogan
Arbeit Macht Frei (Work Makes One Free). Though many of the Jews and
political prisoners at Dachau were forced to work, most of them were
exterminated by the Nazis before they could be liberated in 1945.
A memorial to those who lost their lives now stands on the grounds.*

1942, Hitler's regime began its "Final Solution" to what was
called the "Jewish Problem." From all over Europe, more than six
million captured Jews were sent to the camps and killed. Millions
of others who resisted Hitler also were murdered in the camps.

THE BEGINNING OF THE END

But from that year, the tide of battle turned against the German
military and its allies, known as the Axis powers. On July 20,
1944, a group of German officers tried to kill Hitler with a hidden
bomb. But the attempt failed, and he was able to carry on the war.

The ruined Kaiser Wilhelm Memorial Church on West Berlin's Kurfürstendamm stands as a reminder of the horrors of war.

By the spring of 1945, however, the losses were too much for Germany to bear. The country had already been invaded from all sides; its cities were in ruins and its armies were surrendering everywhere. The Allied powers—especially Great Britain, the Soviet Union, and the United States—were in control. On April 30, just as the Soviet armies were smashing through the last defenses in the German capital, Hitler killed himself in his Berlin bunker.

Eight days later, Germany surrendered unconditionally, thus suffering its greatest defeat in history. The country was little more than a pile of rubble. Its conquerors divided the ruined land into four zones. One was controlled by the Soviets; the other three were governed by the British, French, and Americans. The military commanders of each zone made up an Allied Control Council, which assumed all authority in Germany. Berlin, in the Soviet zone, was jointly administered; each of the occupying nations oversaw one fourth of the city.

THE POTSDAM AGREEMENT

As the Allied military powers were setting up their administration, their political leaders, except for those of France, met in Potsdam, near Berlin, to work out arrangements for Germany's future. The resulting Potsdam Agreement changed the prewar German frontiers a great deal.

The country lost almost one fourth of its former territory. Northern East Prussia went to Russia. The remainder of East Prussia, Silesia, and part of Pomerania and Brandenburg were given to Poland. Ethnic Germans were expelled from Eastern Europe.

The refugees found new homes throughout the rest of Germany. Today you might find Silesians living in Bavaria and Pomeranians in homes along the North Sea.

There were other terms to the Potsdam Agreement. Germany had to promise not to rearm, and the National Socialist party was disbanded. Control of the economy no longer rested entirely with the government, and Germany's political system was to be rebuilt along democratic lines.

These terms meant different things to different nations. The Allied powers did not really agree as to exactly what was the best course to take. France, Britain, and the United States supported the formation of a parliament. They wanted to restore a free press, the right to a fair trial, and other civil liberties. They also supported free enterprise. The Soviets objected, preferring a socialist state.

THE BERLIN AIRLIFT

Cooperation among the four powers ended by 1948, when the Soviets left the Allied Control Council. For ten months in 1948 and 1949, Berlin was cut off from the Western zones in a Soviet attempt to gain control of the city. The Berlin Air Lift broke the Russian blockade. The West flew in supplies over the heads of the Soviet troops and the Russians ended the blockade in May of 1949.

ONE COUNTRY BECOMES TWO

The three Western nations decided that it would be impossible to work with the Soviets in setting up a unified Germany. So they proposed that a national constitution be worked out, with delegates from the various German states. This parliamentary council met on September 1, 1948. Konrad Adenauer, former mayor of Cologne, was elected president of the group. By May of 1949, these politicians had drawn up a constitution, called the Basic Law, for what was to become the Federal Republic of Germany.

It was hoped that eventually this legal system would be used even in the Soviet zone. Today, decades later, that hope still has not been fulfilled.

In the summer of 1949, the first members were officially elected to the *Bundestag*, the new parliament. Adenauer became the first federal chancellor. The three Western occupying powers had the final say-so in German affairs at first. But that power was gradually eliminated. On May 5, 1955, the Federal Republic was given total control over its territory.

The German Democratic Republic (GDR) was founded in the eastern sector on October 7, 1949. The GDR rulers claimed that they were the only Germans still working for unity. They blamed the West Germans for betraying the cause of nationalism.

Thus, since 1949, there have been two German nations. Through the 1950s and 1960s the question of reuniting the two Germanys was seriously discussed on both sides. But neither government was willing to give up its political and economic systems for that of the other.

THE BERLIN WALL

East Germany's standard of living remained much lower than West Germany's. In 1953, strikes and riots erupted in East Berlin (the Soviet section) and other cities in the GDR. Russian tanks and soldiers crushed the revolt. Refugees fled by the thousands to the West. Three million left between the end of the war and 1961. In August of that year the Russians erected a concrete and barbed-wire wall between East and West Berlin.

The Berlin Wall and other border fortifications remain as visible symbols of a divided Germany. Even today, anyone who tries to cross the death strip between the two Berlins might be shot by the East German border guards.

"The German Question," as the Germans call this difficult situation, is still discussed; but the problem is slowly being resolved, or at least covered over. There are still many differences between East and West Germany, despite their common language, trade agreements, and the fact that almost 40 percent of the people in the West have relatives living in the East. It remains difficult for citizens of the GDR to visit the West.

GERMANY TODAY

During the 1970s, both sides came to accept the idea that the two Germanys would remain separate. By the end of the decade, East Germany had established diplomatic ties with 120 nations, including the three Western powers. In 1973, East and West Germany signed a treaty calling for closer cooperation between them.

The West Germans have been taking a more independent course in European and Western Alliance affairs. In 1981, for example, when martial law was declared in communist Poland, the West Germans did not support the United States demand that economic sanctions be leveled against the Soviet Union.

There also has been a growing peace movement in West Germany. Hundreds of thousands have taken to the streets to protest the Western Alliance's wish to set up nuclear missile sites on their soil. They are very much afraid that their nation will be the future battleground between the world's two superpowers, the United States and the Soviet Union. In recent years, the governments of the two Germanys have been cooperating more on various levels, regardless of what their respective allies think. But the territorial split remains, and coexistence is still fragile. Today West Germany must make its own way through this maze of economic, social, military, and political difficulties. What will happen in the future is anybody's guess.

West Berlin

Chapter 5

PLACES TO REMEMBER

Berlin remains the focus of the German spirit, although it is a city divided. The Berlin Wall—a hundred miles of fortifications erected by the East German government—separates East Berlin and West Berlin. West Berlin is a free city, unlike the eastern section of town, which is the capital of the German Democratic Republic (GDR). Berlin is not officially a part of West Germany, nor is it governed by the Federal Republic. Still, Berlin has close ties to West Germany. It sends deputies to the legislature in Bonn, which is now the capital of West Germany, although Berliners do not have full voting powers.

Berlin lies about 110 miles (177 kilometers) inside the GDR. Three air routes, three railroad lines, three highways connect Berlin to the outside world. The entire city encompasses some 350 square miles (906 square kilometers) of which 55 percent belongs to the West. About 1,900,000 people live in the Western sector and 1,100,000 in the Eastern.

This division is really nothing new, Berliners will tell you. In fact, eight hundred years ago, what is now Berlin was two separate municipalities near the Spree River. The trading town of

Kölln was on an island in the middle of the river, and a settlement called Berlin was on the riverbank. In 1307, the two rivals agreed to have a joint magistrate.

Many wealthy businesspeople settled there over the years, and their riches attracted thieves and cutthroats. It took a Hohenzollern prince to chase out all the bad characters and give Berlin a bit more respectability by the 1500s. Over the next centuries, Berlin was the bright light of Germany. It was the intellectual as well as the industrial center of the country.

After World War I, Berlin was reorganized. Territories consisting of eight former independent municipalities, fifty-nine villages, and twenty-seven estates were joined to form one major city, the second largest in Europe, after London. The arts and culture flourished in Berlin until the rise of Hitler and World War II. During that time, this cosmopolitan community became a Nazi power center.

Allied bombing and shelling destroyed most of Berlin during the final days of the war. Today, most of the rubble has been cleared away. But the shell of the Kaiser Wilhelm Memorial Church has been left standing as a reminder of the horrors of war. Berliners, who are famous for their wit and use of nicknames, call the church tower the "hollow tooth"; the new church buildings alongside it are tagged the "compact and lipstick" because of their shapes.

The major street in West Berlin is the Kurfürstendamm, shortened to Ku'damm by the natives who flock to its outdoor cafes, nightclubs, and theaters. More than a hundred coffeehouses line the boulevard. It seems as if no one ever sleeps along the Ku'damm because the clubs remain open most of the night. It is a very popular gathering place for Berlin's young adults.

*The Kurfürstendamm (above) is West Berlin's major street.
The city's hundreds of outdoor cafes always attract crowds.*

Aerial view of the Tiergarten, West Berlin's huge park and zoo

In front of Schöneberg Town Hall, in the American sector of the city, is John F. Kennedy Square, named after the American president who was assassinated in 1963. Earlier that year, he had visited Berlin and delivered a speech at the Berlin Wall. In it, he announced, *"Ich bin ein Berliner"* ("I am a Berliner"). The speech made him immensely popular among residents of the city.

The Tiergarten, a huge park in the British sector of the city, supposedly has one million trees. It's a popular recreation spot among Berliners. The city's seventy thousand dogs enjoy visiting there as well!

The Berlin Wall was built primarily to stop the drain of people from East to West that began at the end of World War II. The average number of refugees was two thouand a day from then until August 13, 1961, when the wall was begun. That is almost one sixth of the total population of the German Democratic Republic.

A sign on the west side of the Berlin Wall warns "Stop—here freedom ends." Above right: Construction of the wall in 1961.

Many West Berlin streets reach a dead end at the wall. The Bernauer Strasse was the site of several escapes when the wall was first put up, through tunnels dug from apartments on the Eastern side. Eventually, all the buildings in the Eastern sector within 50 to 100 yards (46 to 91 meters) of the wall were torn down. At various points in West Berlin, there are observation platforms that overlook the East. The East German border guards stare back at those who climb the towers for a view of East Berlin.

The Brandenburg Gate is in East Berlin just outside the British zone.

Behind the wall, in the middle of the wide clearing of booby-trapped land that is watched by the Vopos, the bricked-up Church of the Reconciliation still stands. The Brandenburg Gate, in East Berlin just outside the British zone, is another famous Berlin landmark. It was once the entrance to the city from the west but is now cut off by the Berlin Wall. Nearby is the Soviet war memorial where tourists watch the changing of the guard.

Just inside the Western zone, near Checkpoint Charlie—one of the crossing points between East and West Berlin—is a museum erected by East German refugees. This little exhibit on the Friedrichstrasse shows the various ways people have used to flee the GDR: armored cars and buses, scaling the wall, and tunneling under it. The boarded-up church and the museum are unofficial symbols of a divided Berlin.

Checkpoint Charlie (above) is one of the crossing points between
East and West Berlin. Goose-stepping East German troops (below right)
guard the Soviet War Memorial (below left) near the Brandenburg Gate.

Munich sights: Aerial view (above left), the beautiful Gothic-style
city hall (above right), and the famous Hofbräuhaus (below).

A patient crowd waits in Munich's Marienplatz for the enameled-copper figures of the city hall Glockenspiel to begin one of the two daily performances in which they move in and out of the archways in a miniature tournament.

CHARMING MUNICH

Things are much brighter in Munich (*München*), the capital of Bavaria. Munich is a very old town—more than a thousand years old, in fact. The third largest city in West Germany, it still retains much of its charm from prewar days. One of the nation's best universities is located in Munich, and the city's museums are famous. It is also a leader in the German publishing and fashion businesses. Many West German industrial companies have their headquarters there.

The carnival lights of Munich's Oktoberfest

The city is best known for its springtime celebration, called *Fasching.* More than a thousand fancy-dress balls and masquerade parties are held between Epiphany and Ash Wednesday. Even the market women take time out to put on costumes and dance in the streets just before Lent begins. Then in the autumn, it's time for more merrymaking at *Oktoberfest.* People from all over the world flock to the city to listen to brass bands and drink beer.

To work off all those pounds gained during the festivals, Munich citizens take advantage of the sprawling Oberwiesenfeld, a stadium constructed for the 1972 Olympics and used for the 1974 World Cup championship soccer matches. All sorts of sports and recreational facilities are available there, from swimming pools to skating rinks.

Hamburg's harbor is one of the largest ports in the world.

HAMBURG: CITY OF COMMERCE

At the opposite end of the country is Hamburg, a city that is also a separate West German state. It lies at the junction of the Alster and Elbe rivers, which join to flow 100 miles (161 kilometers) to the North Sea. Hamburg has always been a favorite trading area because of its location. It was one of the major Hanseatic cities during the Middle Ages and it retains that characteristic even today. Hamburg has one of the largest ports in the world, with more than 12,500 dockworkers available to handle cargo. More than 54 million tons (49 million metric tons) of merchandise flow through the port annually.

The lights of Hamburg—at dusk (above) and along the Reeperbahn (below)

The city was destroyed by massive bombing raids during World War II. But today, Hamburg citizens are proud of their city's beautiful reconstruction.

Several dams block the flow of the Alster River so that it puddles out into a huge lake in the center of town. It's easy for suburban workers to commute by sailboats and dock almost next door to their downtown office buildings. In the winter, many Hamburgians even ice-skate to work over the frozen river surface.

Since Hamburg is such a major trading center, many foreign countries have set up consulates to handle business between their nations and West Germany. Dozens of overseas companies also have offices in the city. Hamburg is a banking, insurance, communications, and trade-show headquarters. The massive Congress Centrum Hamburg, the city's main convention hall, hosts business exhibits and industrial expositions throughout the year.

Catering to all these visitors are wild and woolly nightclubs along the Reeperbahn, or "Rope Street." In the early days of sailing ships, ropes were made and sold here. The street became the dividing line between the "nice" part of town and the rowdy port. A "creep of the Reep" is still a favorite pastime for sailors who enjoy the bars, dance halls, and arcades.

There are some four thousand restaurants in Hamburg, catering to the two million residents and many out-of-towners.

One of the world's best hotels—the Vier Jahreszeiten—is on the lakeshore in Hamburg. Breakfast can be served in the rooms, and is always accompanied by fresh flowers and fruit. Antique furniture fills every room. The hotel even has large thermometers in each bathroom, so guests can check their bathwater temperature.

BONN: CAPITAL CITY

Bonn, the capital of West Germany, is a lovely city on the west bank of the Rhine River. This is another ancient town, dating back more than a thousand years to Roman times. The old quarter and university area lie at the heart of the city today.

Bonn was always a major trading center, and rich merchants built massive homes along the river front. Today, many of these buildings have been turned into government offices.

The city might not have as much nightlife and sparkle as Berlin, Munich, or Hamburg. But it is still an important city because of its political function. The *Regierungsviertel* is the federal government district. In this area, on the site of an old teachers' college, is the *Bundeshaus,* or parliament.

This legislature is divided into two houses: the *Bundesrat,* the upper chamber whose members are appointed by the ten "Länder," or West German states, and West Berlin; and the *Bundestag,* the 496-seat lower house, elected by the citizens of West Germany.

Not far away is the presidential palace. The president is the head of state, whose duties are to represent the Federal Republic internationally and to appoint or dismiss the federal chancellor and ministers. The actual leader of the government is the chancellor, who is chosen in a vote by the members of the Bundestag, the lower house.

The most famous site in the city, however, is not necessarily the government quarter. It's probably Ludwig van Beethoven's home at Bonngasse 20, now a museum. The famous composer was born there in 1770. He lived in Bonn until 1787, when he went to Vienna, then the center of the music world.

Above: The government quarter of Bonn, the capital city
Below: As is true of most West German cities, outdoor cafes
play an important part in the daily life of Bonn residents.

Two views of Frankfurt, the busiest of all West German cities

FRANKFURT: TRANSPORTATION CAPITAL

Frankfurt is the busiest of all West German cities, the hub of all commercial airline flights, ground transportation, and railways. Before the war, giant airships called zeppelins, which looked like floating cigars, set out from here on round-the-world and transatlantic flights.

The modern airport, with its two-mile-long runways, serves thirty million passengers annually. The city's rail station has twenty-four individual tracks, handling hundreds of trains each day.

The region was inhabited some four thousand years ago, in the late Stone Age. The Romans built a fort here two thousand years ago. During the thirteenth century, all of Europe flocked to Frankfurt's trade fairs. A hundred years later, the Holy Roman emperor chose the city's St. Bartholomew's Cathedral as the site for his coronation. Frankfurt has long been a major commercial city, basically because it grew up on a ford on the Main River. It was easy for merchants to cross the river at this point, and was a natural place to build inns, taverns, and warehouses to accommodate the travelers.

Frankfurt's banks were very important in European history. They even lent money to the United States during the Civil War. Ironically, a bomb dropped from an American airplane blew up one of those major financial institutions barely eighty years later, during World War II.

Frankfurt has always been a major political center for free-thinking people. The city resisted Prussian attempts to take over the country in the last century, and its citizens were leading opponents of Hitler's regime.

Cologne Cathedral (top left) dominates the view of the city from the Rhine River. Construction of a "Rheingarten" (top right) has already begun. The park along Cologne's Rhine waterfront will contain a bandshell and outdoor cafes. Vehicle traffic will be diverted to an underground tunnel. Above left: This modern apartment building in Stuttgart contrasts sharply with the old building in Oberammergau (above right), which has been decorated with painted Biblical scenes.

Many other West German cities could tell equally interesting stories: Trier, Speyer, Worms, Mainz, Cologne (Köln), Lübeck, Rothenburg, Baden-Baden, Regensburg, and hundreds of others. They each have something special to offer—industrial might, cultural life, historical drama, or simple friendliness.

Other interesting towns and cities of West Germany include Rothenburg (top), whose medieval walls and towers still remain; Heidelberg (center left), with its famous castle; Passau (center right), at the confluence of the Danube, Ilz, and Inn rivers; and Regensburg (left), one of the country's thousand-year-old cities.

Industry along the Saar River

Chapter 6

WEST GERMANY'S ECONOMIC MUSCLES

The West German economy is closely tied to that of the rest of the Western world. From the grim aftermath of World War II, the country has built itself up like a weight lifter. Now, only four decades after the nation was left a smoldering ruin, West Germany is one of the strongest industrial countries in the world.

The United States and other nations helped Germany regain its strength with massive amounts of financial aid immediately after World War II. It was considered very important to assist this former enemy, so that the problems of the 1920s would not arise again. Today West Germany can stand proudly again, secure in the knowledge that it wisely used that financial help. As a highly industrialized country, it exports mostly finished goods, especially those that take technical skill to produce.

THE RUHR: INDUSTRIAL CAPITAL

In addition, West Germany is very lucky to have many natural resources hidden beneath the countryside. Coal and iron have

Molten iron being poured into a steel-making furnace at a Krupp steel mill

been mined in the Ruhr region for hundreds of years. The Ruhr, in the western part of the country along the border with France, is also the principal steel-manufacturing region of Germany.

Nowhere else in West Germany are there as many large cities clustered so close together as in the Ruhr. Some, such as Recklinghausen, have medieval roots. Oberhausen, on the other hand, grew up with the German railroads. Then there are Dortmund, Essen, Duisburg, and Herne—each with its large factories.

The Germans have been careful to preserve the old-fashioned character of their cities. Although many were damaged during the last war, they have been rebuilt to look much as they did years ago. There are few, if any, large areas of ugly, abandoned land around the coal mines. The refuse from the mines is often used to fill the empty shafts. The re-covered surface is then planted with trees.

The communities housing the Ruhr's workers and miners were

Workers at a Siemens plant learn about a modern toolmaking machine.

planned very well. Instead of crammed slums, they have parks, open spaces, and neat homes.

The chemical and oil-refining industries in the Ruhr have expanded since the end of World War II, opening important new markets for West Germany. In addition, more than half of the nation's electric power comes from Ruhr generators, fired by the district's coal.

West Germany, like most European nations, has to import crude oil. It depends on oil produced in the Middle East and South America. It also has to bring in natural gas and has been working on a pipeline that will transport this important energy source from the Soviet Union.

WORKING MEN AND WOMEN

Industrial production in West Germany has exploded over the past few decades. The machinery-building industry employs the

Production of motor vehicles is one of the country's most important industries.

largest number of people, followed by electronics, heavy industry (coal mining and steel making), chemicals, motor vehicle and aircraft construction, textiles, and food processing.

Because there are never enough skilled West German workers, many men and women from other countries move to Germany to work. Turks, Greeks, Italians, Spaniards, Portuguese, and Yugoslavs make up most of the foreign work force. They are called *ausländische Arbeitnehmer,* or foreign workers. Young people from other countries come to Germany and send part of their wages home to help their families. After a while, some marry and settle in their adopted country. Many German cities have large numbers of foreigners in some sections of town. You might hear more Turkish than German spoken in certain West Berlin neighborhoods, because Turks make up more than 45 percent of that city's foreign population.

The foreign workers receive the same pay and benefits as do the locals. But their presence has created some social problems. Integration proceeds slowly; a few Germans look down their noses at the outsiders.

West Germany must export most of its goods. The country is

A smiling waitress at an outdoor cafe in Munich serves her customers steins of beer, the national drink of Germany.

dependent on trade with other nations. But it is also a leader in sending aid to the poorer countries of the Third World—the developing nations in Africa, Asia, and South America. It is there that the West Germans recognize their markets of the future. West Germany is also a member of the European Economic Community, an organization to promote trade among most of the European nations.

BEER: THE NATIONAL DRINK

Germans enjoy relaxing after a rugged day in the factory or office. Almost everyone agrees that a frothy glass of beer hits the spot. According to statistics, every man and woman in Germany drinks almost 34 gallons (129 liters) of beer every year. Of course, that's just an average. Not everyone drinks that much, and some drink more.

German youngsters like to hear the folk story about the legendary German king named Gambrinus, who supposedly invented beer. However, archaeologists claim that the ancient Egyptians also made this drink. Regardless of who was the first, the Germans have been making beer for hundreds of years and influencing standards of brewing all over the world.

There are many different kinds of beer, from light, golden pilsner to heavy, dark-brown bock beer. In days gone by, many cities had their own breweries. But many of the older breweries have gone out of business over the past few years or have been purchased by larger companies. Still, there are plenty of places that produce German beer. Berlin, for instance, has eight breweries. Recently, the Schultheiss Brewery there celebrated its 130th anniversary.

There's a story about how bock beer began in Germany. Originally, it was made by brewers in Einbeck, a small northern village, way back in 1248. According to local tradition, the neighborhood folks wanted a special beer with which to celebrate the arrival of spring. Only the best ingredients were chosen, and the beer was aged in underground caves. The finished drink was so delicious that the demand for Einbeck beer grew and grew.

In German, *bock* means "goat." Since the legendary King Gambrinus always traveled with a goat, that long ago Einbeck beer was nicknamed *ein bock*—and eventually, simply "bock beer."

Wine is also a popular beverage in West Germany. The country produces more than 70 million gallons (265 million liters) of wine yearly. Huge vineyards lie in the Rheinland-Pfalz, between the Ahr Valley on the north and the Moselle River on the south. The Romans cultivated grapes in the same area; Trier used to be a summer resort for the Roman emperors.

The grape harvest along the Palatinate's "wine road," a string of villages near the German-French border, always provides an excuse for a party. Each fall, little towns celebrate with carnivals,

Terraced vineyards along the Rhine River

band concerts, and plenty of food. Long tables fill the town squares, and everyone tries to sit on the benches closest to the musicians. All around the square are little booths that sell various kinds of wine. Colorful flags and banners fly everywhere over the cobblestone streets. The vineyards on the slopes of the Neckar River near Stuttgart also produce excellent wines, but most of it is consumed locally. The people who live there know they have a good thing!

MEATS, FRUITS, AND VEGETABLES

Although the Federal Republic is able to grow many kinds of vegetables, fruits, and grains, it is not really an agricultural country. The number of people working on farms has declined steadily over the past ten years.

After World War II, almost 25 percent of the entire population was involved in agriculture. Today, barely 8 percent raise crops or livestock. The number of farms also has decreased. The remaining farms, however, have grown larger, and the yields have increased dramatically because of better farming practices and equipment. Today's average West German farmer supplies enough food for thirty of his countrymen.

The eating habits of the Germans have changed over the past forty years. The people eat more fresh fruit, vegetables, and meat, while the amount of potatoes and bread they consume has declined. Still, the Germans love munching on the more than two hundred varieties of breads, rolls, buns, biscuits, and other delicious delights produced by the nation's bakers. A good German baker is worth a ton of gold.

While West Germany imports oranges from Spain and hams from Poland, it exports many other items: cattle for slaughtering, work animals and breeding stock, grain, potatoes, sugar, seeds, beer, wine, milk, cheese, eggs, and fish products.

CRAFT WORK

Handicrafts form a very important part of the West German economy. The number of craft workers has remained fairly stable since World War II. More than 600,000 large and small businesses employ four million people to make all sorts of items, many for export.

The Black Forest villages of Furtwangen and Triberg have museums of highly prized antique clocks. The cuckoo mechanism was invented about 1730 by Franz Kletterer of Schönwald. He devised two wooden whistles and a bellows activated by the clock mechanism to announce the time. It was a great hit, and eventually everyone in the neighborhood seemed to be making clocks.

Today's cuckoo clocks, of course, are made in factories, where machinery does most of the work. Clock insides are now metal instead of wood. If it weren't for the international market, there probably wouldn't be a cuckoo-clock business in Germany at all. More than 80 percent of the funny little timepieces are shipped out of the country. Of the remaining 20 percent, most are purchased by tourists in souvenir shops from Garmisch to Wittingen.

Bavarian wood carvings are known worldwide for their intricacy. Some communities, such as Oberammergau, are especially famous for this craft. In that city, more than 250 wood-carvers turn out items that range from gift-shop trinkets to massive murals. The best works are labeled *handgeschnitzt*—a guarantee of quality, designating that the piece is hand carved.

Oberammergau has a government wood-carving school. Americans, Japanese, Africans, and many other people come to learn from the experts. The school is free, but the students have to agree to remain in Oberammergau and work for three years.

Before anyone can open a wood-carving shop, he or she must work with a master carver for at least five years. The apprentices are paid per piece and by the size.

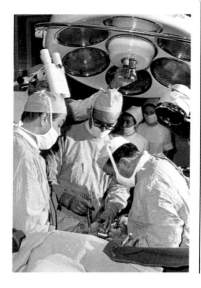

Most employees in West Germany are covered by health insurance. This surgical team is operating at the University of Saarbrücken.

INVESTING IN PEOPLE

Virtually all employees in West Germany are covered by union agreements. Average annual wages in the early 1980s ranged between $17,500 for skilled manual laborers and $24,000 for white-collar workers. The standard workweek is forty hours. Almost everyone is covered by a social security plan that was started by Bismarck in the 1880s. The plan provides health insurance (introduced in 1883); industrial accident insurance (1884); old-age, survivor, and disability pensions (1888); and unemployment insurance (1927).

In return for contributions that are deducted from paychecks, a worker may ask the government for assistance. Every worker in West Germany who is laid off from a job has the right to be trained for a new position. All insured persons and their families are entitled to free medical, hospital, and specialist treatment and a good wage plan if they are injured on the job or get sick.

Although the Federal Republic spends 26 percent of its gross national product on social services, it does not consider itself a welfare state. This assistance is considered an investment in people.

Almost 86 percent of the work force belong to one or another of the seventeen unions in the largest German labor organization, the *Deutsche Gewerkschaftsbund* (DGB). It is therefore fairly easy to negotiate wages and avoid union rivalries. The DGB metalworkers union, with 2.7 million members, is the largest union in the world. It covers the entire West German iron and steel industry, the car firms, shipbuilding and engineering, the electronics companies, the computer and atomic industries, and more.

There are many different employers' organizations on regional and local levels, many of which belong to the umbrella group known as the German Employers' Association.

The West Germans have a very interesting way of dealing with their bosses. It's called *Mitbestimmung* or "co-determination." This means that workers can participate in the running of the factories.

The rule allowing co-determination, called the Works Councils Act, was passed in 1920. At that time, workers' representatives took positions on the boards of German companies. The Nazis crushed the labor union movement in the 1930s, but it came back powerfully after the war. Today, workers participate on two levels—on the shop floor and in the boardroom of the firm. A typical company works council deals more with hiring and firing, wages, employment policies, and so on, than with the actual management of the company.

Naturally, due to personalities and conflicts within a firm, there are still labor disputes. In fact, there were many strikes in 1978, when West German industry was hit hard by an economic slump. But generally, the councils have helped in the discussion of important matters and have actually prevented many potential labor problems.

West Germany will continue as a major economic power. It is a forward-looking country, eager to learn new ways of operating its factories and farms. The Federal Republic is not afraid of the future. It has plenty of muscle to flex on the world market.

Germany has produced some of the greatest composers in the history of the world. One of the greatest was Ludwig van Beethoven (left), who was born in Bonn in 1770. Johannes Gutenberg, born in Mainz about 1400, invented printing from movable type. A replica of his printing press (below) can be seen in the Gutenberg Museum in Mainz.

Chapter 7

LAND OF CULTURE
AND ACTIVITY

Beethoven! Wagner! Gutenberg! Few other countries have as rich a cultural history as the Federal Republic of Germany. Literature, painting, architecture, theater, opera, music—each of the arts has its own passionate following among the Germans. The diversity of all these forms is staggering. One author, asked to describe the extent of German culture, wrote, "It's rather like being called upon to comb the fur of a mammoth with a toothbrush."

The German constitution guarantees freedom of art and scholarship, of research and teaching. It also gives primary responsibility for cultural promotion to the individual West German states: Bavaria, Baden-Württemberg, Saar, Rhineland-Palatinate, Hesse, North Rhine-Westphalia, Lower Saxony, Schleswig-Holstein, Bremen, Hamburg, and the city of West Berlin.

The diversity of German art forms is rooted in history. From the Middle Ages on, each locality developed its own lively cultural scene. Up until the late nineteenth century, there were numerous German principalities and kingdoms. Each had its own theatrical troupe and opera company, as well as resident artists, architects, and craft workers. Each duke tried to outdo the neighboring baron. So they all had magnificent palaces, concert halls, parks, and museums. The bishops and the monasteries, the rich businesspeople and the free cities, all supported the arts.

The establishment of the empire in 1871 didn't change the belief that the localities could best promote the arts. But the fourteen years of the Weimar Republic after World War I were too confusing and frantic to produce much of a central German art scene. The Nazis had a devastating impact on German culture. Any creative person with an independent thought wound up dead or imprisoned or had to flee to a safe place.

After the war, however, the intellectual and artistic community came back stronger than ever. Damaged buildings were repaired. Festivals were restarted. Literary prizes were awarded again. The West Germans regained confidence in themselves when they saw the renewal of what they had known and loved.

MUSIC LOVERS

In music, the Germans have never been bothered by national frontiers. Ludwig van Beethoven from the Rhineland and Johannes Brahms from Hamburg both lived and worked in Vienna during their most creative periods. Franz Liszt was born in Hungary and moved to Weimar. Other musicians moved about in the same way, bringing all sorts of influences from different areas into their compositions.

Eighty symphony orchestras in the Federal Republic now

The city of Würzburg (above) hosts an annual Mozart festival

receive financial help from local or state governments. Then there are numerous radio orchestras, private theaters and cabarets, and community orchestras in what seems like every small village.

The many music festivals in West Germany attract visitors from all over the world. The Richard Wagner Festival, started in Bayreuth in 1876, is still popular. There's a Mozart festival in Würzburg, one for Beethoven in Bonn, and another for Handel in Göttingen.

Opera is the main attraction at Hamburg; a concert hall there dates from 1678. There are major festivals in Munich and Wiesbaden. Organ music is popular at Nuremberg, while jazz is king in West Berlin. Pop concerts are held in meadows, town squares, beer halls, and in open-air theaters. Wherever West Germans gather, they seem to want music.

COMEDY AND TRAGEDY

Approximately eighty-five city and state theaters receive help
from their local governments. But that doesn't include the many
amateur theater companies and traveling troupes that have
revived the seventeenth- and eighteenth-century custom of
playing on portable stages anywhere they can: juvenile centers,
prisons, courtyards, senior citizen homes. The theatrical message
is thus spread to nearly everyone in West Germany.

In the late 1960s, there were several companies called Free
Theater Groups, including the Beetroot Collective, the Red Heads,
and the Ruhr Cultural Cooperative. These were basically political
troupes, and they came up with all sorts of wildly creative stage
presentations.

West Berlin, Munich, Hamburg, Cologne, Frankfurt, Stuttgart,
Ulm, Bochum, and a few other cities have some of the best
resident companies and theatrical programs of any in the Federal
Republic.

Puppet theater has always been popular in Germany.
Documents have been found that describe puppet plays performed
in 1175. Germany often has been called the classical country of the
art of puppetry. Scholars have collected the names of more than a
thousand puppeteers who have worked in Germany over the past
four hundred years! There is now a professional puppeteers'
association that sponsors programs for both children and adults.
In Brunswick, an International Puppet Theater Week takes place
every three years. There is an annual puppet festival in Bochum.
Some of the intricate puppets are bigger than real people, and
some are very tiny. But all are fun to watch.

There are also theaters for child audiences and theaters with child actors in West Germany. Often during the summer, troupes visit playgrounds and parks to put on shows for youngsters. Excellent plays for young people have been written by well-known authors such as Friedrich Karl Waechter. He has a popular character called Superman Kiebich, who always seems to get into trouble. Kiebich's friend Dutz and the children in Waechter's stories always save the poor hero.

COPING WITH THE PAST

West German theater also has its serious side. Since the war, playwrights have faced the problem of dealing with the Nazi blemish on their country. Some of their works have shocked outsiders.

Rolf Hochhuth's *The Deputy* (1963) denounced Pope Pius XII for not saving more German Jews during Hitler's rule of terror. A later play, *Soldiers,* talked about the bombing of German cities during the war. Some of the plays of Bertolt Brecht also tackled the question of the Nazi days.

The West Germans have a word for their concern about the Hitler era. They call it *Vergangenheitsbewältigung.* This means "coping with the past."

As part of this process, many young Germans have gone to Israel to help on farms there. They have assisted the Jewish families who moved to that country after the war. The Federal Republic also has paid money to people who suffered under the Nazis. A number of Germans who worked for Hitler and his storm troopers have served prison terms.

Novelists and poets have discussed Hitler as well, often asking how he could have come to power so easily. Günter Grass,

Heinrich Böll, and Alfred Andersch are among the better-known authors who have dealt with this question.

Today's writers have urged their fellow Germans to learn from their terrible past. They consider it a grim, unwelcome chapter in their history. But now they seem to agree that it is time to move on. Their works are ready to be added to the long list of distinguished German authors, many of whom were philosophers as well: Immanuel Kant (1724-1804); poet and dramatist Johann Wolfgang von Goethe (1749-1832); Friedrich von Schiller (1759-1805); Heinrich Mann (1871-1950) and his brother Thomas (1875-1955); Franz Kafka (1883-1924), and hundreds of others.

BOOKS FOR CHILDREN

Children's literature is very important in West Germany. About two thousand new picture books, nonfiction books, craft books, and novels are published every year. Exhibitions of children's books are often held, with programs that include games, theater productions, and conversations with authors and artists.

An international showing of children's books is held every year in the Ruhr city of Duisburg. The town has many creative youngsters as well. Twenty of them recently developed a series of "touch" books for their blind friends; another group wrote a detective story focusing on Duisburg.

FINE PRINT

West Germans read a great deal: while riding on a bus, traveling on a boat, or waiting in an airport terminal. There are nearly 500 daily newspapers in the Federal Republic, most of them politically independent. There are also student newspapers, weekly papers, and special trade journals. In addition, the average German can choose from among 12,500 different magazines published in the country. Journalists are well respected in the Federal Republic.

West Germans are proud that European printing actually got its start in their country. Johannes Gutenberg, who lived in Mainz in the 1400s, is believed to be one of the first Europeans to print with movable type. Before Gutenberg, most books were written by hand, with quill pens on parchment paper. His work enabled printed material to be produced faster and better. There are several major museums dealing with printing, newspapers, and typesetting in Mainz, Offenbach, and Aachen.

A COUNTRY OF MUSEUMS

The Germans' love of their heritage is reflected in the care they give to preserving art treasures and architecture. The early princes considered painting and sculpture important for keeping up their images. Impressive art collections were put together all over the country. It's the same today. There are more than fifteen hundred museums in the Federal Republic, with about three hundred in North Rhine-Westphalia alone. Art from all eras is respected equally.

There are also many specialty museums in the Federal Republic. Munich has a beer museum; there is a wine museum in Speyer, hunting museums in Berlin and Darmstadt, the Museum of Playing Cards in Bielefeld, transportation and toy museums in Nuremberg, postage stamp museums in several cities, a Museum

West Berlin's Egyptian Museum and Greek Museum

of Dolls and Puppets in Neustab, the Museum of Tobacco and
Cigars in Bünde, a violin museum in Mittenwald, and more.

During World War II, most of the collections were stored in safe
places. But the museum buildings themselves weren't as lucky.
Allied bombing destroyed many of them, and the West Germans
had to rebuild. Many of the new structures look very modern. But
some were reconstructed in the older style, so there is an
interesting mix of architecture in many parts of Germany.

THE MEDIA

Youngsters from the Alps to the North Sea enjoy visiting the
museums, but they also like watching television. They can see

shows from the United States, such as "Sesame Street," with words in German. Favorite West German children's programs are "That's What You Think," "The Suburban Crocodiles," and "News From Uhlenbusch." These shows deal with all sorts of topics, from what youngsters think of grown-ups to a behind-the-scenes look at a movie studio.

The West German film industry is very active. The most popular movies seem to be Westerns, with German-speaking actors playing American cowboys and Indians. For more serious productions, the federal government has established a Center for Films for Children and Young Adults.

Radio stations involve young people by inviting entries in playwriting competitions. Some talk shows feature children discussing different topics.

SCHOOL DAYS

West German youngsters can't watch television or films all day. They do have to attend school. Children three to six years old can go to kindergarten if their parents wish; however, they must begin formal school when they are six years old. Primary school lasts for four years. After that, young people go on either to a secondary school *(Hauptschule)*, where they can receive some job training; an intermediate school *(Realschule)*, which is sort of a vocational school; or a high school *(Gymnasium)*, which leads to university classes. About 12.5 million West German youngsters attend school; many go on for higher degrees and certificates. Schools and textbooks in the Federal Republic are free.

Advanced students can attend a university or technical college, a teacher training college, art or music academies, or a polytechnic. Polytechnic schools specialize in science, business, management, social work, or engineering. Young people need a certificate of graduation, called *Abitur*, from the lower schools before being admitted.

There are plenty of adult education classes for older people who want to return for more studies.

Children of foreign workers also must go to school, although it is often hard to persuade them to get a higher education. Only about half obtain a graduation certificate from the secondary-school level. The foreign children attend classes with German youngsters and then take extra lessons in their native language.

AN EQUAL CHANCE FOR EVERYONE

The West Germans are very concerned about mentally or physically handicapped children. They want to give all children an equal educational chance. West Germany provides many special programs and classes for the deaf, blind, and others in need of assistance. Of course, many of these youngsters don't need to attend a special school. They are visited by therapists in their regular schools. A recent television series, "Our Walter," described the life of a handicapped boy and showed children what it is like to have physical difficulties.

George Kostja, a rock-and-pop music expert who works for Bavarian Radio in Munich, has been working on a pet project for handicapped youngsters. He has set up a "Rock House" for kids who can't get around easily. The Rock House features concerts and similar musical shows. It is open to everyone. Kostja, who is physically handicapped himself, thought this would be a good way to bring all kinds of boys and girls together.

Children on summer holiday play in a public pool in Speyer.

PLAY TIME

No matter where children go to school in West Germany, vacations are fun and exciting. All youngsters have a long summer holiday, lasting about six weeks. Many towns have organized play programs in the parks. Hanover, for instance, offers a "holiday pass" for a small fee. It enables children to participate in more than forty different activities all summer — from visits to the library and zoo to open-air theater. Munich has a "holiday on the outskirts" program that includes two-week visits to area farms, day trips to the mountains, and outings to swimming pools. West Berlin's media center offers youngsters summer courses in learning to make films and operating a radio station.

Soccer and sailing are two favorite sports in West Germany.

If you want to start a conversation with a German young person, bring up sports. Almost everyone is involved in some sort of club or team. Soccer is a favorite game. There are forty-two sports associations under the umbrella of the German Sports Federation. The German Gymnastics Association has two million members. One of its clubs—the Hamburg Turnerschaft—was founded in 1816.

West German youngsters love rafting down the Isar River from Wolfratshausen, south of Munich. The four-hour ride includes a lunch stop and plenty of swimming time. Another exciting trip is a twenty-mile raft trip on the Lahn River from Bad Ems, just east of Koblenz. The vessel passes many castles and quaint villages of the Rhineland-Palatinate.

Young sailors enjoy outings on the North Sea and the many inland lakes of the Federal Republic. In addition, tennis, fishing, and horseback riding are popular sports. Hiking is another inexpensive way to get exercise. Youngsters like to collect small metal badges as souvenirs from villages and parks along the way. They nail the little symbols to their ornately carved walking

Mountain climbing in the Bavarian Alps is exciting and dangerous.

sticks. It is then easy to see where a hiker has been, just by looking at the staff. Bookshops in every district sell hiking maps with well-marked routes.

It's always fun to visit the local zoo. West Germany's "safari parks" have some impressive wildlife collections. Siberian tigers are big attractions in the Zoological Park in Berlin's Tiergarten. More than four thousand animals live in natural surroundings in Munich's 170-acre (69-hectare) Hellabrunn Zoo. Its children's section, the Kinder-Tierpark, features performing monkeys. Trained chimpanzees also can be seen at Wilhelma Park in Stuttgart. There are stone dinosaurs and a rabbit village at Hamburg's Hagenbeck Animal Park.

Many American-style theme parks also are springing up in West Germany: Fort Fun, Hansa-Land, Phantasieland, Schwalmtal, and dozens of others. They have carnival rides, theatrical shows, trained animals, and games. From the arts to the outdoors, the Federal Republic has plenty of things to keep young people active.

*Young Germans are among the leaders of the growing peace movement in Europe.
This group is participating in an anti-nuclear demonstration in Bonn.*

Chapter 8
THOSE GERMAN WAYS

As is true of every country, West Germany has its own customs and traditions. But the world is changing quickly for German young people, much as it is everywhere else. There are issues today that nobody dreamed of only a short while ago. Young Germans are among the leaders of the growing peace movement in Europe. They are aware of the need for a clean environment. They want to have good educations that lead to secure jobs.

A few years ago, the newspaper *Welt am Sonntag* asked thousands of West German young people whom they most admired. Topping the list were mothers and fathers, followed by Jesus Christ. Next came rock singer Elvis Presley, then rocket scientist Werner von Braun, old-time comedy film star Charlie Chaplin, former West German Chancellor Helmut Schmidt, Albert Schweitzer—who worked as a medical doctor and missionary in Africa, soccer star Franz Beckenbauer, assorted singers, writers, and others. Adolf Hitler headed the list of the least-admired adults.

Nationalism, the feeling of being proud of one's country, is not such an important factor in Germany anymore. Prior to World

War II, it was the accepted thing to feel that Germany was the most powerful nation in the world. Now, many talk about a United Europe, with each country being a separate state. Young Germans are among the most traveled of all Europeans, which helps them understand what is happening in other nations. They love their vacations and spend weeks abroad—camping, driving, hiking from Scandinavia through the Middle East to Africa and even through South America and the Orient.

It is often easy to become dissatisfied with things at home, especially when it comes to finding a job in a country that has its share of economic problems. A university degree sometimes isn't enough to guarantee a good job. There are more than a million students in higher education, and that means a lot of competition. West German youngsters have questions about women's roles in society, about dating and raising families, about the threat posed by nuclear weapons, how to protect their land from pollution—all the same worries that other young people have. Some young West Germans have taken out their frustations by joining terrorist groups. But the majority seem willing to work within their political system to achieve what they feel is important.

So the Federal Republic is faced with the challenge of dealing with all these factors. West Germany, like the rest of the world, is experiencing the clash of old ways and new.

GERMANS IN AMERICA

West Germans have always been reflective people. They work hard and they play hard. They are willing to work their way through difficulties. These attributes are important exports. Wherever Germans go, they seem to take these qualities with

West Germans work hard, but
they also know how to relax.

them. Germans have played a part in American history from its beginning. Three German shipwrights—Unger, Keffer, and Volday—belonged to the crew of the ship that brought the first English colonists to Jamestown, Virginia, in 1607. They stayed in the settlement to help build cabins, putting their construction skills to use. During the American Revolution, more than thirty thousand German soldiers fought for the king of England in the colonies. England's George III, the head of the House of Hanover, was able to persuade many of his German relatives and friends to send their troops—for a price. But hundreds of German soldiers deserted to the American army, and more than twelve thousand remained in America after the war. One of the most famous soldiers of the Revolution was the Prussian General Friedrich Wilhelm von Steuben, who trained the colonial army during the winter at Valley Forge. Over the ensuing years, many other Germans—famous and unknown—went to America.

Since those early years, Germans have taken their place in American society. Among other things, Germans have given Americans wieners, sauerkraut, pretzels, Christmas carols, Easter egg hunts, and blue jeans.

Blue jeans? Sure enough. A Bavarian immigrant named Levi Strauss landed in San Francisco during the California gold rush in 1850 and opened a hardware store. He heard miners complaining that their pants tore apart too easily. So Strauss made some trousers from canvas. Soon "Levi's pants" were known all over the American West.

After the German revolution of 1848 failed, many revolutionaries fled to other countries. They carried their spirit with them to South America, particularly to Chile, and the United States.

At the end of the nineteenth century, tens of thousands of Germans went to the United States. Most were skilled craft workers of all kinds.

Many distinguished people fled Hitler's Nazi regime in the 1930s and 1940s because of their political and religious beliefs. Some of the most famous settled in the United States.

A PROUD ROLE FOR GERMAN WOMEN

The German traditions of public service, of courage, and of artistic achievement certainly are not limited to men. The Roman historian Tacitus was the first to talk about the high esteem in which Germans held women. Throughout the Middle Ages, there were famous women doctors, heads of religious orders, and artisans. In the mid-nineteenth century, the German Women's Movement spearheaded the drive for better schools and improved working conditions. During World Wars I and II, millions of women had to leave their homes to work in factories.

The reconstruction of West Germany after World War II was due in large part to women's hard work. In fact, there is a large monument in West Berlin dedicated to the *Trümmerfrauen*, the women who cleared away all the rubble and debris in the destroyed city.

It was not until 1918, however, that German women won the right to vote and could be elected to office. The constitution of 1919 gave them equal rights with men. But it is obvious that even in today's work force women often do not receive the same responsibilities and the same pay as men in similar jobs. Nearly ten million women have jobs outside the home in the Federal Republic, and they are slowly gaining more recognition. Many more are winning administrative and managerial positions in industry and with the government, although there is still a long way to go. Older men and women in West Germany still believe, by and large, that women belong at home. Today's forward-looking young Germans, however, have put that out-of-date attitude to rest.

Women have been very prominent in the arts. Marie Luise Fleiger has written excellent plays. Her style has been copied by numerous young playwrights. Textile designer Anka Krohnke is well known for her beautiful colors and patterns. Ursula Scheid is a noted potter, and Brigitte Klosowski is an excellent jewelry maker. Contemporary women novelists in West Germany include Ilse Aichinger, Marie Luise Kaschnitz, Angelika Mechtel, Karin Struck, Gabriele Wohmann, and many others. These women are bright lights on the West German cultural scene.

POLITE BEHAVIOR

Some traditions don't fade easily in West Germany. Many standards of politeness still must be met. German children are expected to behave and be quiet, especially in the company of adults. Certainly it doesn't always work that way. But generally there is strict discipline in German families. The father rules the roost—or at least thinks he does. Some German mothers still teach their daughters to curtsy when greeting grown-ups. Little boys are supposed to bow when saying hello to adults. But many modern West German teens consider these mannerisms silly.

When West Germans visit each other, they are very formal. An invitation to a West German home is a very special expression of friendship. Visitors should always bring a bouquet of flowers;

usually an uneven number, such as five or seven, is given to the woman of the house. A bottle of wine is also a nice gift if families are getting together for an evening meal.

It's always proper to arrive right on time. In West Germany it's considered impolite to be more than ten or fifteen minutes late for an appointment, unless there is a good reason for a delay.

GOOD TASTE

One of the things that may startle foreign guests is the way West Germans eat. Whenever they eat something that needs cutting, such as a piece of meat, they follow the European custom of holding the fork in the left hand and the knife in the right. They keep the utensils that way for the whole meal, using the fork to push food against the blade of the knife. It looks confusing at first but once you know how it is very simple.

When adults get together for a meal or a night out, they often have wine or beer. There is much clinking of glasses and mugs. The usual toast is *"zum Wohl!"* which means "to your health." Another popular toast is *"prost,"* or "cheers."

West Germans usually eat a light breakfast, consisting of soft-boiled eggs, hard rolls with butter and jam, and coffee, tea, or milk. For those with heartier appetites, there may also be fruit and a plate of cold meats and cheese. Most Germans enjoy a hot meal at noontime in a restaurant or company cafeteria. German sandwiches are usually open faced and are eaten with a knife and fork. For snacks, sausages are best. A hungry German can choose from hundreds of varieties of *Wurst.* Each type of sausage can be made in several different ways. Bratwurst, for instance, can be fat, white, spicy, plain, or a dozen other styles. Bockwurst is long and

An array of German food is displayed at a Munich hotel (left). Lebkuchen, German cookies frosted with sweetheart sayings, are sold during Oktoberfest.

red, like a giant hot dog. The *Frankfurter* is skinny and usually sold in pairs. There are also hundreds of kinds of cheese that go well with German sandwiches.

The fast-food restaurant business is slowly creeping into West Germany. Young Germans enjoy spending time at McDonald's restaurants, but a more popular chain is the *Wienerwald*.

Discos, teen clubs, and arcades are great gathering places for West German young people. For the adults, *Weinstuben* are cafes where wine is served, along with hearty snacks or complete meals. *Brauereien* and *Bierkeller* are restaurants that feature a special brand of beer with their meals.

A *Konditorei* is a pastry shop. Don't go in if you are on a diet. The goodies served there are guaranteed to add pounds to your figure. Think of butter cake topped with *Schlagsahne* (fresh whipped cream). Dream of a chocolate torte, dripping with frosting and cherries. Yum. Then think again and go for a hike.

West Germans enjoy relaxing in open-air sidewalk cafes, glass enclosed in the winter. A visitor can sit at a table for hours,

West Germans enjoy relaxing in open-air beer gardens such as this one in Munich.

sipping, reading, talking, or just watching the passing crowds. The German coffee served by these establishments is quite strong. Each cafe has a huge coffeemaker, with mysterious knobs, dials, and steam valves that somehow pressurize the coffee. The resulting drink has a lot of flavor; the aroma is just as rich as the coffee.

Beer gardens offer the wares of the country's famous breweries. These are lots of fun to visit, with their long tables, community singing, and dancing.

Adults can gamble in one of the nineteen legal *Spielbanken* in the Federal Republic, operated by the finance departments of the various states. A *Spielbank* is a casino, with roulette wheels, card games, dice, slot machines, and other devices designed to gobble money. Going into a *Spielbank* at Garmisch-Partenkirchen, Baden-Baden, Lindau, or West Berlin is like stepping into a spy film. Often, the men dress in tuxedos; women wear flowing gowns and glittering jewels. Of course, some people are more casually dressed. But everywhere is the click-click and flutter of the wheels and the flash of money.

On Autobahnen, such as this one in the Ruhr area, there is no speed limit.

ON THE ROAD

Germans love to travel. A major highway is called an *Autobahn*. While crossing the Federal Republc, cautious drivers learn to stay far to the right on the roadway. There is no speed limit on the *Autobahnen*, and some West Germans love to zoom past slower vehicles. Tailgating and weaving in and out of traffic are not uncommon. For years West Germans were considered among the most aggressive drivers in Europe. But that is not the case any more. Drivers are learning to be more courteous. They have to be—there are millions of other cars and trucks on the road, plus bicycles, farmers' carts, motorcycles, buses, and all sorts of other vehicles. These latter obstacles are encountered more often on the narrow side roads called *Landstrassen*. A motorist has to be very alert while driving in West Germany.

The Deutsche Bundesbahn trains are clean, fast, efficient, and safe.

The West Germans are proud of their national airline, *Lufthansa*, which flies to the world's major cities. The carrier has some of the most modern planes available, with one model nicknamed the "air bus." Businessmen and women enjoy flights aboard these special planes that fly to other European countries.

While it is very easy to get in and out of the Federal Republic by air, it is also sensible to take the train. The *Deutsche Bundesbahn*, the German Federal Railroad, is clean, fast, efficient, and safe. Special *Autoreisezüge* even carry rail passengers' private autos. The traveler can then make long-distance trips with a minimum of gas use and fuss. Vendors provide food and drinks when trains stop at stations. You can reach out a window, buy what you need, and have a quick snack without leaving the train. Taking the train is advisable even when a traveler does have an automobile. The main stations are always in the heart of the city, close to the local information office, hotels, museums, shops, and similar attractions. Taking the train beats paying for an expensive cab ride.

A crowded Oktoberfest beer tent in Munich

HOLIDAY FUN

West Germans often ask themselves, "Why go anywhere at all? We have everything right here!" When the conversation rolls around to that debate, the Germans are usually talking about the wealth of festivals and traditional feasts they have in their own backyards.

Munich, of course, has *Oktoberfest* and *Fasching.* Other cities and districts also have their holiday fun.

The most impressive religious feasts are in the Catholic areas of the country. There the feast of Corpus Christi is one of the most

Left: An Easter-egg tree displays a colorful assortment of eggs.
Right: Parades are part of the fun during Oktoberfest.

important events. Along the Rhine, on the lakes of Chiemsee and Staffelsee, crowds gather in their national costumes and celebrate with huge floating processions. On the Friday following the feast of the Ascension of Christ, the city of Weingarten in Upper Swabia is the setting for a parade of more than two thousand horsemen carrying banners and flags to the local cathedral. Many cities celebrate the feast of St. Leonhard, the patron of animals, with parades featuring cows, pigs, and horses accompanied by whip-cracking drovers and herders in bright outfits.

The Thirty Years' War was one of the worst periods in German history. Many festivals recall that terrible time with plays and

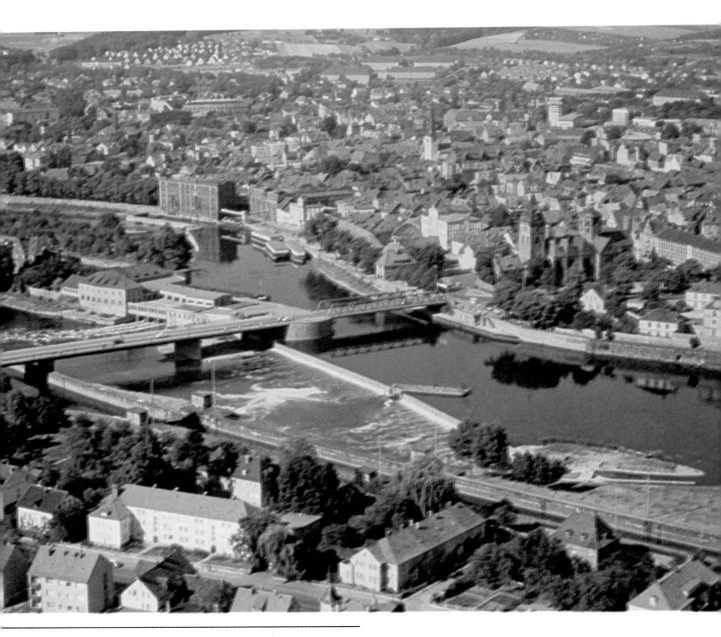

The legend of the Pied Piper is reenacted on summer Sundays in the city of Hamelin, now called Hameln.

dioramas. Rothenburg, a city on the Tauber River, has a "camp life" demonstration each year. The entire city population dresses in clothes of that period and acts out the events of the war— without the bloodshed, naturally.

The folk tale "The Pied Piper of Hamelin" is reenacted every Sunday from June to August in the city now called Hameln. The famous story of the angry piper who lured away the children from town does have a basis in history. Many German children left their homes in 1284 to participate in the Children's Crusade, a religious march against the Moslems in the Holy Land. None of the children ever returned; thus was the folk tale born.

On April 30, in Bad Harzburg, people dress in witch and demon costumes for a wild program called *Walpurgisfeier*. This event recalls ancient pagan days in Germany, but now it is celebrated in good fun.

During these festivals, the German love of a good time really comes through. Bavarians are noted for the *Schuhplattler*, a rowdy dance in which the men slap their leather shorts, or *Lederhosen*, and the women twirl in billowing skirts. The *Watschentanz* is a dance in which boys punch each other in mock fights to get the attention of girls. Other districts have similar dances.

A GERMAN CHRISTMAS

No other holiday has such a far-reaching effect on West Germany as does the celebration of Christmas. By the time the leaves begin to fall in autumn, children are already excited. St. Martin's Day, November 11, is the official beginning of the Yule season. On the evening before that feast, children carrying lanterns through the streets are followed by bands and other marchers. The program honors a soldier who gave part of his cloak to a beggar, who turned out to be Christ, according to the legend. Huge bonfires are lighted all over the country as a reminder that winter soon will be coming. Gifts also are exchanged.

Children also celebrate the feast of St. Nicholas on December 6. Santa Claus is patterned after this historical figure, who was actually a bishop from Myra, a city in Asia Minor. An adult dressed like a bishop rides through the villages on St. Nicholas Eve, attended by a character carrying a bag of gifts. This attendant is called Ruprecht. He is supposed to spank bad youngsters as well as reward good ones.

In some areas of prewar Germany, especially in Prussia and Pomerania, other folk figures would ride through town at Christmastime. They would be dressed in goatskins, straw, and old clothes and demand gifts for themselves. These creatures probably originated in pre-Christian days to represent demons and other evil beings.

Christmas markets do a brisk business right up to Christmas Eve. Little booths set up in the town squares feature all sorts of holiday crafts, toys, games, and ornaments. On Christmas Eve all the shops close exactly at 1 P.M. Everyone hurries home to get ready for Christmas Eve supper, which is followed by church services. Every home has a beautifully decorated Christmas tree and a crib scene. Christmas Day is celebrated with delicious cakes. A roast pork or a goose dinner is served, along with baked apples. There are few things that smell better than a German house at Christmastime.

On New Year's Day, children receive good luck coins, usually a *Pfennig* (penny) under their dinner plate.

Christmas is one of the most important holidays in West Germany. The tradition of decorating evergreen trees during this season originated in Germany.

German ways are certainly fascinating. Even as some traditions change or are dropped because of the pressures of the present, the basic German spirit of the past stays as strong as ever.

An asterisk (*) refers to the approximate location of a place that does not appear on the map.

MINI-FACTS AT A GLANCE

GENERAL INFORMATION

Official Name: Federal Republic of Germany

Capital: Bonn

Official Language: German. At present, the standard and written form of German is based largely on High German, which was spoken originally in the southern and central uplands of Germany. Low German, spoken in the northern plains, can still be heard in some farm areas.

Government: West Germany is a federal republic. Citizens over the age of eighteen may vote. The legislature is divided into an upper and a lower chamber. The *Bundestag,* the lower chamber, has 496 members plus 22 from West Berlin, all elected to four-year terms. The *Bundesrat,* the upper chamber, has 41 members plus 4 from West Berlin. Members are appointed for indefinite terms by the ten *Länder,* or states, and West Berlin. The president is head of state. His duties are mainly ceremonial. He is an elected official and serves a five-year term. The chancellor is the head of government. He is chosen by the members of the *Bundestag.* He also can be removed from office by the *Bundestag.* The chancellor selects the ministers who make up the cabinet and head the various government departments.

Flag: Black, red, and gold in three equal horizontal stripes are the colors of the flag of the Federal Republic. The colors date from the days of the emperors in the Middle Ages. They reappeared in the war against Napoleon when a corps of army volunteers drawn from all the German principalities wore black uniforms with red braid and gold buttons. Subsequently, German students who believed in a unified country used the colors on their banners. In the first attempt to create a democratic Germany, the leaders of the 1848 revolution adopted the tricolor flag. However, the flag was not used until 1918, when the German national assembly of the Weimar Republic officially adopted it. When Hitler came to power, he got rid of the tricolor and used his own flag, a red banner with a black swastika on a white circle. The swastika was originally a good luck symbol from the Far East. In 1950, the tricolor was again designated the official flag.

Coat of Arms: A black eagle with red beak and claws on a gold background is the Federal Republic's coat of arms, its national symbol. The eagle was originally used as a symbol by the Romans. After the decline of Rome, the eagle reappeared on the shields of kings. Charlemagne, the first Frankish king to unite the various German tribes and other Europeans, had the statue of an eagle placed atop his palace in Aachen. A double-headed eagle remained the seal of the German and Holy Roman emperors after Charlemagne's kingdom broke up. In 1848, the double-headed eagle was revived as the symbol of German unity. When Germany was finally unified in 1871, a single-headed eagle was placed on the coat of arms. In 1919, the eagle became the seal for the Weimar Republic and was restored in 1950 as a symbol of tradition and history.

National Song: Third stanza of *"Deutschland-Lied"* ("Song of Germany")

Religion: About 49 percent of the West Germans are Protestants; most of this group belongs to the Lutheran church. Approximately 45 percent of West Germans are Roman Catholics.

Money: The basic unit is the Deutsche Mark (DM). There are 100 Pfennig (Pf.) to the Mark. Coins are 1 Pf., 2 Pf., 5 Pf., 10 Pf., 50 Pf., 1 DM, 2 DM, and 5 DM. Paper bills are 5, 10, 20, 50, 100, 500, and 1,000 DM. In 1982 one Deutsche Mark was worth about 40¢ in United States currency.

Weights and Measures: West Germany uses the metric system.

Population: 60,839,000, including West Berlin (1988 estimate). Distribution is 86 percent urban, 14 percent rural. The density is 635 persons per sq. mi. (245 persons per km²).

Cities: (1988 official estimate)

West Berlin	1,860,100
Hamburg	1,579,884
Munich (München)	1,266,549
Cologne (Köln)	916,153
Essen	619,991
Frankfurt	595,348
Dortmund	572,094
Düsseldorf	561,686
Stuttgart	561,628
Bremen	526,377
Hanover	508,298

GEOGRAPHY

Land Regions: There are four main land regions in West Germany. From north to south, they are (1) the Northern Plains, (2) the Central Mountains, (3) the Southern Hill Country and the Black Forest, and (4) the Bavarian Alps.

Borders:
North—Denmark, the North Sea, the Baltic Sea
South—Austria, Switzerland
West—The Netherlands, Belgium, Luxembourg, France
East—East Germany, Czechoslovakia

Highest Point: Zugspitze, 9,721 ft. (2,963 m)

Lowest Point: Sea level

Rivers: Major rivers include the Danube, Elbe, Ems, Oder, Rhine, and Weser. The Danube River is the only major river in Germany that flows eastward.

Lakes: Many lakes found throughout West Germany were formed by ancient glaciers from the Alps.

Mountains: The Bavarian Alps, part of the largest mountain system in Europe, rise more than 6,000 ft. (1,800 m). The Black Forest is also a mountainous region; its average peaks rise between 2,500 and 3,000 ft. (762 and 910 m), with some as high as 4,000 ft. (1,200 m). The South German hills rise from about 500 to 2,500 ft. (150 to 762 m).

Forests: Forests cover nearly 30 percent of Germany. Two thirds of the forests consist of firs, pines, spruces, and other cone-bearing trees. Other trees include beeches, birches, and oaks.

Climate: The climate is mild. The average temperature in January, the coldest month, is about 30° F. (-1° C). The hottest month, July, has an average temperature of 70° F. (21° C). There is approximately 20 to 40 in. (51 to 100 cm) of precipitation a year.

Greatest Distances: North to south—562 mi. (900 km)
East to west—250 mi. (400 km)
Coastline: 354 mi. (570 km)

Area: 96,005 sq. mi. (248,651 km²), including West Berlin

ECONOMY AND INDUSTRY

Principal Products:
Agriculture: Livestock, dairy products, potatoes, barley, oats, rye, sugar beets, wheat, grapes for wine making
Fishing: Shrimp, cod, herring, redfish
Manufacturing: Steel, automobiles, cement, clothing, electrical equipment, processed foods, metal, cameras, leather goods, scientific instruments, toys, wood pulp, paper
Mining: Coal, iron ore, lead, petroleum, potash, rock salt, zinc

Communications: There are nearly 500 daily newspapers. The *Bild-Zeitung* of Hamburg is the largest. About 12,500 different magazines are published in West Germany. Most West German homes have a radio and more than half have a television set. The radio and television stations are owned by the government. Commercials are broadcast at only a few special times during the day. Everyone who owns a radio or television set must pay a monthly license fee to support the networks. The postal, telegraph, and telephone systems are owned by the government.

Transportation: The railroad, for the most part, is owned by the government and consists of about 18,000 mi. (29,000 km) of track, which connects all parts of Germany. There are also approximately 94,000 mi. (151,000 km) of roads across West Germany. This includes 2,800 mi. (4,510 km) of four-lane highways known as *Autobahnen.* There is no speed limit on the *Autobahnen.* West Germany has about 13 million automobiles, 3.5 million buses, trucks, and other commercial vehicles, and 230,000 motorcycles. The Rhine River and its branches are extremely important in water transportation .The rivers are connected by a system of canals. The inland waterways are used by about 7,000 ships. The seagoing merchant fleet is made up of about 2,000 ships. Hamburg and Bremen are the major seaports. Deutsche Lufthansa is the government-owned airline. There are 11 commercial airports in West Germany. West Berlin is connected to West Germany by railroads, highways, canal systems, and air corridors.

EVERYDAY LIFE

Food: The main meal in Germany, generally served at noon, might consist of veal or pork and vegetables such as beets, carrots, onions, potatoes, or turnips. A soft-boiled egg, rolls, and jam, served with coffee or milk, usually make up a breakfast. A light supper, served in the evening, might consist of bread, cheese, and sausage.

Housing: West Germany still suffers from a housing shortage, and rents remain high. Most people live in apartment houses. Few people own homes, since land is very expensive.

Holidays: Official holidays include New Year's Day, Good Friday, Easter, Pentecost, Labor Day (May 1), and Christmas. In Catholic areas, the Feast of Corpus Christi (celebrated eleven days after Pentecost) and All Saints' Day (November 1) are important events. Lutheran areas celebrate Reformation Day (October 31) and Repentance and Prayer Day (third Wednesday in November). In addition, many cities have various feasts and festivals.

Culture: The Federal Republic has 200 theaters and opera houses, 100 large orchestras, and 1,500 museums. Most of the theaters and opera houses rely on subsidies from the state and local governments. German music and drama festivals are praised throughout the world for their quality. Some of the best known are the Wagner festival at Bayreuth and jazz festivals in Berlin. In addition to the many chamber orchestras, there are 80 symphonies. Nearly 50,000 new books are published each year in West Germany. Popular writers often have their works translated. As an example, Nobel Prize winner Heinrich Böll's writings have been translated into 35 languages.

Sports: The most popular sport in Germany is soccer, called *Fussball*. Other favorite activities including skiing, hiking, canoeing, rowing, sailing, and swimming. Sharpshooting is also popular.

Schools: Education is free and is controlled by the state government. Every child between the ages of six and fourteen must attend school. All children spend four years at primary school *(Grundschule)*, followed by either five years at secondary school *(Hauptschule)*, six years at intermediate school *(Realschule)*, or nine years at high school *(Gymnasium)*. Pupils finishing secondary school usually become apprentices for three years so they can learn a trade. Intermediate school helps young people prepare for jobs in business and administration. The graduation certificate *(Abitur)* from the high school qualifies a student for university studies. There are 195 universities and other institutions of higher learning in West Germany, as well as more than 25 art and music academies. The total student population at colleges and universities numbers nearly 1 million and includes 54,000 foreign students. Tuition is free. The 1980 literacy rate was 99 percent.

Social Welfare: The Federal Republic has an extensive system of social security and welfare. It covers old-age pensions, unemployment and sickness benefits, allowances for injury, rent, and child care, as well as grants for education and job training. About one third of the gross national product of West Germany is spent on social security.

CITIES OF WEST GERMANY

It is easy to tell the origin of German cities by studying their names. Many town names in southern Germany end with *heim* (Mannheim, Rosenheim). This means they were settled by Frankish people. The ending syllable *furt* (as in Frankfurt) means the town grew up around a ford, a place where travelers could wade across a river. If town names end or begin with *reuth, reut, reute, rode,* or *rath* (Bayreuth, Reutlingen), this means space for the original village was hacked out of a forest *(roden* in German).

Many towns in southern and western Germany were founded by the Romans. All names ending in *weiler, weier, wihl,* or *weil* (Appenweier, Rottweil) came from the Latin word *villa,* meaning house. The ending *kastel,* as in Bernkastel, stems from the Latin word *castellum,* or castle. If a town name ends with *burg* (Hamburg), the town grew around a German castle, a *Burg.*

Towns originating around abbeys or monsasteries still carry the term *Kloster* (cloister) or *mönch* (monk), such as Klosterreichenbach and München. A name containing *zell* means that the "cell," or home, of a hermit was nearby.

Town names ending with *ingen* (Sigmaringen) are usually in Swabia and those with *ing* in Bavaria. In fact, the name Sigmaringen shows that the city was founded by a German named Sigmar and his "kin," or relatives.

In Germany, the free cities were very important. In the old empire, these communities were not subject to the prince ruling the surrounding countryside (Augsburg, Frankfurt, Ulm, and many others). They were responsible only to the emperor, who often visited them for months at a time. All free cities developed a long heritage of trading and culture. Only two of the original fifty-one free cities have remained independent—Hamburg and Bremen—both of which are city-states and are represented in parliament.

IMPORTANT DATES

1000 B.C.—Tribes from northern Europe begin to arrive in present-day Germany

A.D. 9—German tribes defeat Roman General Varus

12—Romans build Castra Bonnensia, which will become the city of Bonn

50—Cologne becomes a resort for Roman veterans

179—Regensburg founded

259—Franks cross the Rhine River

768—Charlemagne begins his wars with other German tribes

800—Charlemagne crowned emperor

843—Treaty of Verdun; empire divided among Lothar (Central Empire), Charles the Bald (Western Empire), and Louis the German (Eastern Empire)

845—Hamburg destroyed by Vikings

870—Cologne's first cathedral built

911—First German monarchy established; Conrad I of Franconia elected king

919—Henry I of Saxony becomes king of Germans

962—Holy Roman Empire established; Otto the Great crowned

1156—Frederick I named emperor; Holy Roman Empire strongest ever

1372—Frankfurt becomes a free city

1386—University of Heidelberg founded

1400s—Reformation movement begins in Bohemia

1438—Hapsburg family of Austria begins almost continuous rule of Holy Roman Empire

1445—Gutenberg perfects letterpress printing

1483—Birth of Martin Luther

1493—Peasants' Revolt

1517—Luther nails up his complaints about the church; Reformation begins in Germany

1524—War of the Peasants

1555—Religious Peace of Augsburg legalizes Lutheran-Roman Catholic split.

1582—Würzburg University founded

1618-48—Thirty Years' War

1648—Hapsburgs defeated; Treaty of Westphalia ends Thirty Years' War; Austria breaks from the empire

1701—Berlin Academy of Sciences founded

1740-86—Frederick the Great consolidates Prussia, makes it a great power

1749—Poet Johann Wolfgang von Goethe born

1806—Napoleon invades, ends the Holy Roman Empire

1812—Brothers Grimm begin collecting fairy tales

1813—Napoleon defeated at Leipzig

1815—Congress of Vienna establishes the German Confederation with thirty-nine sovereign states; Otto von Bismarck born

1824—Ludwig van Beethoven composes his Ninth Symphony

1833—German Customs Union (the *Zollverein*) founded

1848—Revolution throughout Europe; German Confederation ended; Karl Marx finishes his "Communist Manifesto"

1849—Thousands of German republicans emigrate to the United States

1850—German Confederation refounded

1862—Bismarck named premier of Prussia

1864—Prussia defeats Denmark

1866—Prussia defeats Austria, establishes the North German Federation; Bismarck named federal chancellor

1871—Prussia and German states defeat France; German Empire (the *Reich*) founded

1876—Inauguration of the Bayreuth Festival

1878—Albert Einstein born

1890—Bismarck ousted as chancellor

1914-18—World War I; Allies defeat Central Powers; German Empire ended

1919—Weimar Republic formed

1921—Einstein wins Nobel Prize in physics

1925—Paul von Hindenburg named Reich president

1932—Six million Germans unemployed

1933—Adolf Hitler named Reich chancellor and becomes dictator; parliament disbanded

1936—Olympic games in Berlin

1938—Austria annexed by Germany; German-speaking areas of Czechoslovakia taken over

1939-45—World War II; Allies defeat Germany; Hitler commits suicide

1945—Germany divided into four military occupation zones

1947—Mass expulsion of Germans from Eastern Europe

1948—Berlin airlift

1949—Federal Republic of Germany founded; Theodor Heuss named first federal president; Konrad Adenauer named federal chancellor

1953—Revolt in the German Democratic Republic (East Germany)

1955—West Germany and East Germany declared independent countries

1961—Berlin Wall erected

1963—Ludwig Erhard named chancellor

1966—K.G. Kiesinger named chancellor

1969—Willy Brandt named chancellor

1970—Treaties signed with the Soviet Union and Poland

1971—Brandt receives Nobel Peace Prize

1972—Olympic games in Munich

1973—Treaty between East and West Germany ratified; treaty signed with Czechoslovakia; Federal Republic and German Democratic Republic become members of the United Nations

1974—Helmut Schmidt named chancellor; World Cup soccer championships in Munich

1980—Peace demonstrations continue across West Germany

1981—Martial law declared in Poland; Federal Republic refuses to join movement to sanction the Soviet Union

1988—France and West Germany establish joint councils on defense and economic issues.

IMPORTANT PEOPLE

Konrad Adenauer (1876-1967), chancellor of West Germany from 1949 to 1963

Ilse Aichinger (1921-   ), contemporary novelist

Alfred Andersch (1914-   ), novelist who deals with subject of Hitler's rise to power

Ernst Barlach (1870-1938), artist, sculptor, playwright, and poet

Max Beckmann (1799-1859), landscape and architectural painter

Ludwig van Beethoven (1770-1827), composer, born in Bonn

Otto von Bismarck (1815-1898), Prussian statesman, first chancellor of German Empire

Gebhard von Blücher (1742-1819), Prussian field marshal

Heinrich Böll (1917-   ), novelist and poet, received Nobel Prize in literature in 1972

Johannes Brahms (1833-1897), composer and pianist, born in Hamburg

Willy Brandt (1913-   ), mayor of West Berlin, 1957-1966; chancellor of West Germany, 1969-74; winner of 1971 Nobel Peace Prize

Bertolt Brecht (1898-1956), playwright and poet, in exile from 1935

Karl Carstens (1914-   ), president of West Germany since 1979

Charles IV (1316-1378), crowned Holy Roman Emperor in 1355; issued Golden Bull in 1356

Karl von Clausewitz (1780-1831), Prussian army officer known for books on science of war, born in Burg

Karl Dönitz (1891-1981), naval commander who planned and commanded U-boat fleet; sentenced as war criminal

Albrecht Dürer (1471-1528), painter and engraver

Adolf Eichmann (1906-1962), Nazi leader convicted and executed in Israel for war crimes

Ludwig Erhard (1897-1977), economist and politician; chancellor of West Germany from 1963-1966

Johann Gottlieb Fichte (1762-1814), philosopher and metaphysician

Marie Luise Fleiger, contemporary playwright

Theodor Fontane (1819-1898), poet, novelist, and essayist

Frederick I, Barbarossa (1123?-1190), Holy Roman emperor from 1152-1190

Frederick William (1620-1688), elector of Brandenburg

Paul J. Goebbels (1897-1945), official propagandist of Nazi Germany, committed suicide

Hermann W. Goering (1893-1946), second in command to Adolf Hitler in Nazi Germany, committed suicide

Johann Wolfgang von Goethe (1749-1832), poet, born at Frankfurt am Main

Günter Grass (1927-   ), novelist and poet who has dealt with subject of Hitler era

Walter Gropius (1883-1969), architect who founded the Bauhaus school to coordinate the building arts

Matthais Grünewald (1465?-1528), painter regarded as greatest representative of German Gothic style

George Frederick Handel (1685-1759), composer, born in Halle

Gerhart Hauptmann (1862-1946), writer and playwright, received Nobel Prize in literature in 1912

Georg Wilhelm Hegel (1770-1831), philosopher, born in Stuttgart

Heinrich Heine (1797-1856), lyric poet and literary critic

Rudolf Hess (1894-   ), Nazi politician sentenced as war criminal

Paul von Hindenburg (1847-1934), general during World War I, president 1925-34, born in Posen

Adolf Hitler, *der Führer* (1889-1945), chancellor and dictator, brought on World War II by invading Poland, committed suicide

Rolf Hochhuth (1931-   ), playwright who has dealt with treatment of Jews in World War II

Hans Holbein the Elder (1465?-1524), historical painter

Hans Holbein the Younger (1497?-1543), portrait and historical painter

Alfred Jodl (1892?-1946), Nazi army officer hanged as war criminal

Uwe Johnson (1934-   ), novelist who deals with the divided Germans

Franz Kafka (1883-1924), poet and novelist

Immanuel Kant (1724-1804), metaphysical and transcendental philosopher

Marie Luise Kaschnitz (1901-1974), novelist

Wilhelm Keitel (1882-1946), Nazi field marshal hanged as war criminal

Kurt Georg Kiesinger (1904-   ), chancellor from 1966 to 1969

Helmut Kohl (1930-   ), elected chancellor in 1982

Gotthold Ephraim Lessing (1729-1781), dramatist and critic

Franz Liszt (1811-1886), Hungarian composer and pianist, lived in Weimar 1848-61

Erich F.W. Ludendorff (1865-1937), general and politician who served during World War I

Martin Luther (1483-1546), father of the Reformation

Rosa Luxemburg (1870-1919), socialist agitator

Heinrich Mann (1871-1950), novelist, essayist, and playwright

Thomas Mann (1875-1955), novelist and essayist

Angelika Mechtel (1943-   ), contemporary novelist

Felix Mendelssohn (1809-1847), composer, pianist, and conductor, born in Hamburg

Ludwig Mies van der Rohe (1886-1969), architect known for his glass-and-steel apartment buildings

Helmuth Karl von Moltke (1800-1891), Prussian military genius important in the building of the German Empire

Friedrich Nietzsche (1844-1900), philosopher and poet

Joachim von Ribbentrop (1893-1946), Nazi diplomat hanged as war criminal

Tilman Riemenschneider (1460?-1531), sculptor and wood-carver

Erwin Rommel (1891-1944), Nazi general, died apparently as result of Hitler's orders

Alfred Rosenberg (1893-1946), Nazi leader and writer hanged as war criminal

Friedrich von Schiller (1759-1805), poet and playwright

Arno Schmidt (1914-   ), contemporary novelist

Helmut Schmidt (1918-   ), chancellor from 1974 to 1982

Arthur Schopenhaur (1788-1860), philosopher, expounder of pessimism

Robert Schumann (1810-1856), composer

Richard Strauss (1864-1949), conductor and composer

Karen Struck (1947-   ), contemporary novelist

Rudolf Virchow (1812-1902), pathologist and political leader

Richard Wagner (1813-1883), composer and writer on music

Kurt Weill (1900-1950), composer of operas, ballets, and musical comedies

Christoph Martin Wieland (1733-1813), poet, prose writer, and translator

Gabriele Wohmann (1932-   ), contemporary novelist

RULERS OF GERMANY

Conrad I	911- 918
Henry I (Henry the Fowler)	919- 936
Otto I	936- 973
Otto II	973- 983
Otto III	983-1002
Henry II (Henry the Saint)	1002-1024
Conrad II	1024-1039
Henry III (Henry the Black)	1039-1056
Henry IV	1056-1106
Henry V	1106-1125
Lothar	1125-1137
Conrad III	1138-1152
Frederick I (Barbarossa)	1152-1190
Henry VI	1190-1197
Otto IV	1198-1215
Frederick II	1215-1250
Conrad IV	1250-1254
[An *interregnum*/ a period between reigns]	1254-1273

Rudolf I	1273-1291	Maximilian II	1564-1576
Adolf	1292-1298	Rudolf II	1576-1612
Albert I	1298-1308	Mathias	1612-1619
Henry VII	1308-1313	Ferdinand II	1619-1637
Louis IV	1314-1347	Ferdinand III	1637-1657
Charles IV	1347-1378	Leopold I	1658-1705
Wenceslaus	1378-1400	Joseph I	1705-1711
Rupert the Elector	1400-1410	Charles VI	1711-1740
Sigismund	1410-1437	Charles VII	1742-1745
Albert II	1438-1439	Francis I	1745-1765
Frederick III	1440-1493	Maria Theresa	(1740-1780)
Maximilian I	1493-1519	Joseph II	1765-1790
Charles V	1519-1556	Leopold II	1790-1792
Ferdinand I	1556-1564	Francis II	1792-1806

House of Hohenzollern as Kings of Prussia

Frederick I	1701-1713
Frederick William I	1713-1740
Frederick II (Frederick the Great)	1740-1786
Frederick William II	1786-1797
Frederick William III	1797-1840
Frederick William IV	1840-1861
William I	1861-1871

House of Hohenzollern as Emperors of Germany

Wilhelm I	1871-1888
Frederick II	1888-1888
Wilhelm II	1888-1918

Weimar Republic

Friedrich Ebert	1919-1925
Paul von Hindenburg	1925-1934

Third Reich

Adolf Hitler	1934-1945

Allied Military Government	1945-1949

German Federal Republic

Presidents

Theodor Heuss	1949-1959
Heinrich Lübke	1959-1969
Gustav Heinemann	1969-1974
Walter Scheel	1974-1979
Karl Carstens	1979-

Chancellors

Konrad Adenauer	1949-1963
Ludwig Erhard	1963-1966
Kurt Georg Kiesinger	1966-1969
Willy Brandt	1969-1974
Helmut Schmidt	1974-1982
Helmut Kohl	1982-

INDEX

Page numbers that appear in boldface type indicate illustrations

125

About the Author

Martin Hintz is one-half German, a heritage from his father's side of the family. His great-grandfather fought in the Prussian army when the powder smoke was so thick that it obscured the other side of the battlefield. Hintz has traveled extensively in West Germany, including West Berlin, covering the political, travel, and sports scenes for numerous magazines and newspapers in the United States. He currently lives in Milwaukee, Wisconsin, a city with a definite Teutonic flavor. The city's sausage works, breweries, festivals, soccer clubs, and interest in Germanic history help keep alive the flavor of the Old Country. His wife Sandy, sons Daniel and Stephen, and daughter Kate share Hintz's love affair with this lifestyle. Hintz, a former newspaper reporter, has a master's degree in journalism.